THE TRIUMPH OF
THE SLIPPERS

PASCAL BRUCKNER

The Triumph of the Slippers

On the Withdrawal from the World

Translated by Cory Stockwell

polity

First published in French as *Le sacre des pantoufles. Du renoncement au monde* © Éditions Grasset & Fasquelle, 2022

This English translation © Polity Press, 2024

Polity Press
65 Bridge Street
Cambridge CB2 1UR, UK

Polity Press
111 River Street
Hoboken, NJ 07030, USA

ISBN-13: 978-1-5095-5952-7 – hardback

A catalogue record for this book is available from the British Library.

Library of Congress Control Number: 2023941413

Typeset in 11 on 13pt Sabon
by Fakenham Prepress Solutions, Fakenham, Norfolk NR21 8NL
Printed and bound in Great Britain by CPI Group (UK) Ltd, Croydon

The publisher has used its best endeavors to ensure that the URLs for external websites referred to in this book are correct and active at the time of going to press. However, the publisher has no responsibility for the websites and can make no guarantee that a site will remain live or that the content is or will remain appropriate.

Every effort has been made to trace all copyright holders, but if any have been overlooked the publisher will be pleased to include any necessary credits in any subsequent reprint or edition.

For further information on Polity, visit our website:
politybooks.com

For Eric and the little devils

"Worse than the noise of boots is the silence of slippers."

MAX FRISCH

Contents

Preface

The Oblomov Hypothesis

Oblomov is a landowner living near St. Petersburg in the middle of the nineteenth century. An honest and upright man, he nonetheless suffers from a natural penchant for inertia. He lives less in his house than on his couch, less on his couch than in his immense oriental robe, and less in his robe than in his "long, soft, wide"[1] slippers. His body is flabby, his hands are chubby, and his movements are all marked by a graceful softness: Oblomov lives lying down most of the time. For him, walking and standing are interruptions of the time he spends in his bed or on his sofa: "When he was at home – and he was almost always at home – he lay down all the time, and always in the same room, the room in which we have found him and which served him as a bedroom, study, and reception-room."[2] Oblomov is the very model of the man who is at once overworked and pusillanimous, for whom simply thinking about what he has to do is a kind of torture:

> As soon as he got up in the morning and had taken his breakfast, he lay down at once on the sofa, propped up his head on his hand and plunged into thought without

sparing himself till at last his head grew weary from the hard work and his conscience told him that he had done enough for the common welfare.[3]

Simply writing a letter takes him weeks, even months, and requires a complex ceremony. Every decision carries a huge psychological cost. His deceptively docile valet Zakhar neglects his work and leaves the house in an unspeakable state of disorder. Some days, Oblomov forgets to get up, opens one eye at about four in the afternoon, and says to himself that anyone else in his place would have already gotten through a lot of work. At this prospect alone, he feels overwhelmed and goes back to sleep. As a little cherub, Oblomov had been overly pampered by his parents, who coddled him like a fragile plant. Indeed, his life had begun with a movement of fading away: "From the very first moment I became conscious of myself, I felt that I was already flickering out."[4]

When his friend Stolz introduces him to a young woman, Oblomov panics. He is terrified by the mere idea of sharing his life with a wife, going out into the world, reading newspapers, and living in society. He falls in love with the charming Olga, who is responsible for making sure he doesn't fall asleep during the day; he goes for long walks with her, but cannot bring himself to take the next steps in their relationship. She teases him, tries to get him to stop napping, and reproaches him for his bumbling and for not being more daring. She calls him a coward, and is driven to despair by this man who even refers to himself as an "old shabby, worn-out coat."[5] Weighed down by pressure, constantly overwhelmed by tiny activities that he never has time to complete, Oblomov ends up leaving her. At the age of 30, he's still getting ready to "start his life."[6] Such is the illness he suffers from: abulia, sleepiness, and procrastination.

"When you don't know what to live for, you live anyhow – from one day to another. You are glad the day is over, that the night has come, and in your sleep you can expunge from your mind the wearisome question why you have lived this day and are going to live the next."[7] Unable to love, to travel, or indeed to take any action at all, he soon stops going out, and sinks down into his pillows until he's submerged by them. His tenant farmer and his relatives shamelessly rob him, stealing the meager resources of his harvest. When he finally moves to smaller lodgings, and falls for his landlady and her lovely white arms, he continues to be swindled, this time by his landlady's brother.

Behind its comedic appearance, Oblomov is a poignant description of the impossibility of existing. The more the hero sleeps, the more he needs rest. Having never known great joy, he has also avoided great suffering. He has kept within himself the light that was searching for a way out – the light that "consumed itself inside its prison house"[8] before being extinguished. Since his desires were never matched by his abilities, he has never forged ahead, because forging ahead "meant to throw the capacious dressing-gown not only off his shoulders but also from his heart and mind."[9] He ends his life by simply settling down "quietly and gradually into the plain and spacious coffin"[10] that he has made for himself, with his own hands.

CHAPTER 1

The Four Horsemen of the Apocalypse . . .

Why think about Oblomov today? Because, minus Netflix and the internet, he was the hero of our lockdowns, and will perhaps also be the hero of the post-lockdown era: the man or woman in bed, during this existence in a hover to which we were constrained for two whole years, was us – was you. The pandemic was a moment of simultaneous crystallization and acceleration, one that consecrated a historical movement that long predated it: the triumph of fear and the paradoxical enjoyment of a fettered life. The pandemic made going into quarantine (whether voluntary or forced) a possibility for everyone, a refuge for fragile souls. Goncharov's novel is perhaps less a portrait of the Russian soul, as Lenin lamented, than a premonition addressed to all of humanity – a literature not of entertainment but of warning. The great books are the ones we read and reread because they shed light on events that they seem to foreshadow, events that come about long after their publication. There are at least two traditions of Russian literature: one of resistance to oppression (Boris Pasternak, Vasily Grossman, Varlam Shalamov, Alexander Solzhenitsyn, Svletana Alexievich), the other of despair and fatalism, and these traditions mirror and respond to each other. One offers unparalleled examples of courage in the face of abomination, while the other focuses on resignation in the face of destiny, or even love of servitude (Dostoyevsky's genius was to reconcile them). In both cases, their ability to enlighten remains unrivaled.

In addition to the tedious tragedy that it represented for billions of people, the Covid emergency has led to a vigorous rekindling of the debate between caution and daring, between nomads and homebodies, between pioneers of the world outside and explorers who remain indoors. The twenty-first century, which began with the September 11, 2001 attacks, continues today with the threat of climate imbalance, the persistence of the coronavirus, and finally the war declared by Russia on Ukraine and Europe – all calamities that foster what we might call the Great Withdrawal. This accumulation of misfortunes has permanently traumatized a younger generation that was raised, in Western Europe at least, with the gentleness of peace and promises of well-being. This generation is in no way ready to face adversity. The end of the twentieth century was a period of openness, from both the standpoint of morals and that of travel. That era is over: the closing of minds and spaces is well under way. We now have space tourism for millionaires but, for most, crossing a border or even leaving one's own home has become problematic. Covid has fallen like a providential star on a Western world that no longer believes in the future and assumes the coming decades will do no more than confirm its collapse. The virus has crowned all these anxieties with the terrible seal of possible death. Yet all it did was reveal our ways of thinking.

The two dominant ideologies in the West today – declinism on the one hand, and catastrophism on the other – have at least one thing in common: *they both speak the language of survival.* The things that compete for our fear today present themselves as absolute priorities, but there is also a competition between visions of the end of the world, which, rather than cancelling each other out, combine nicely: we have the choice between dying as a result of disease, extreme heat, attacks, or enemy bombs. To parody one of Churchill's quips about the Balkans: for the last 20 years, we have been subjected to more history than we can consume. Our time is an exciting one, no doubt, but painfully so.

In this regard, how many people experienced the return to normalcy as a shock? At first, they found the prohibitions restrictive; later, they found the lifting of these prohibitions distressing. Won't they miss the nightmarish imprisonment that they wholeheartedly cursed when it was decreed? They are like those prisoners who, once released, sigh as they reminisce about the bars of their cell – prisoners for whom freedom has the bitter taste of anxiety. They're ready to seize upon any excuse to cloister themselves once more. Their bedroom and house are microcosms that suffice in and of themselves, so long as they are kitted out with the latest technology. Voluntary self-confinement in the face of a dangerous world – the dungeon without walls, chains, or guards that people freely choose – should be feared far more than lockdowns imposed from above. The jailer is in our own heads. This period of life in slow motion has sanctioned an impressive easing of social constraints: limited contact, restricted outings, gatherings cut short, work from home, absent bosses, life in a bathrobe or pyjamas, authorized sloppiness, splendid regression. The disruptive or tempting Other has disappeared or been kept at a distance. Some experienced this cooping-up as a form of pleasure: the curfew, the muzzle-like mask, the safety precautions, and the "two-meter society" annoyed us, but it also gave us boundaries. We went from claustrophobia, the fear of confinement, to agoraphobia, the fear of open spaces. The pandemic worried us, but it also freed us from a greater worry: the problem of freedom. It is possible that this freedom will acquire, in the years to come, the bitter taste of a memory or of a chimera.

Who could have foreseen that this experience of being behind closed doors would, by and large, be viewed charitably – almost as a long vacation – by a substantial number of those who lived through it? Many argued in favor of what one might call a sporadic lockdown or a conditional opening. Countless people in France and other European countries no longer wish to return to the office, instead dreaming of a simple life in the midst of nature, far from the noise of cities and the upheavals of History. The end of carefree living goes hand in hand with the triumph of negative passions. We now define ourselves by subtraction – we want to consume less, spend less, travel less – or by opposition, by what we are against: we're anti-vax, anti-meat, anti-voting, anti-mask, anti-nuclear, anti-vaccine-passport, anti-car. Meanwhile, in medicine, the term "negative" – not being infected by AIDS or the coronavirus – has taken on a salutary meaning, while "positive" has become synonymous with potential suffering. Unbeknownst to us, the pre-pandemic world was already in its death throes when Covid began. It's true that, since the lockdown ended, bars and restaurants have been taken by storm; impatient crowds are champing at the bit to live again; frenzied tourists are pouring in to experience something new, even if it means flooding train stations and airports; people are protesting in solidarity with victims of war – and this is a good sign. Life means excess and profligacy or it ceases to be life. But the pandemic gave a strategic advantage to the forces of stunting. Our future hinges on the tension between these two camps.

Our opponents – hateful slavophiles, radical Islamists, Chinese communists – denounce Western decadence, viewing it as the dominance of minorities coupled with unbridled materialism and the progress of unbelief. Many of us have long since formulated this diagnosis, but in a balanced way. Neither the recognition of the struggle of women and homosexuals, nor the weakening of blind faith, nor the guarantee of a certain level of comfort are in themselves factors of decline: on the contrary, they are marks of civilization. One can criticize the excesses of emancipation (as in the case of wokeism) without renouncing it. Who would want to live in Vladimir Putin's Holy Russia or in an Arab or Muslim country under Sharia law – not to mention Xi Jinping's totalitarian China? But it is true that the legitimate protection we enjoy in Western Europe, and especially in France, often degenerates into chronic dissatisfaction, a hand-out mentality that is always disappointed: whatever the State does, it is never enough, and the help it provides makes us weaker and leads us to mistake annoyances for tragedies. The proliferation of rights is accompanied by an equal decrease in duties, opening the door to endless demands. I am owed everything, without having to give anything back in return. Just look at the protests, and indeed the riots, of those who objected to the pandemic measures. In the name of freedom, they insisted on being allowed to do what they wanted when they wanted, while also demanding that public authorities look after them if problems arose. Leave me alone when everything is fine, take care of me when it's not. The modern patient is an *impatient patient* who is irritated by the limits of medicine ("incurable" is the only truly obscene word in our vocabulary), but also suspects it of having ill intentions or of being backed by shady financial interests. The more the progress of science accelerates, the more exasperation grows in the face of its flaws and delays: we cure so many diseases, so why can't we cure them all? From a simply rational standpoint, it is astonishing that so many citizens have risen up in rage against the very thing – vaccination – that was supposed to save them (or at least protect them), going so far as to assault or even threaten to kill doctors and nurses. Some people were so relentless that they continued to curse vaccines at the very moment they were dying in hospital beds because they refused the injections that would have saved them. Better dead than vaccinated!

The pejorative way we speak of "the pre-pandemic world" – as if it had been a depraved era – suggests that the pandemic was seen by many as an ordeal of moral purification. The asceticism and even puritanism of some camps found their prejudices confirmed by this ordeal. Some will always feel best in the streets, in packed trains: these are people driven by the instinct for discovery and the hunger for horizons. But a different tendency could come to prevail if the hydra of fear wins out: the triumph of enclosed spaces and those who huddle within them. When people feel disenfranchised because of the way the world is moving forward, there is always a strong temptation to fall back on what is most familiar. "It may not be much, but I make do with what I have" – such was the petty bourgeois wisdom of the twentieth century. Far from disappearing, the pandemic will be normalized as we integrate it into our list of everyday nuisances. It will remain just virulent enough to worry the anxious, and not quite deadly enough to disturb the carefree. But it's only one item in the long list of misfortunes that afflict us, and it drags behind it the hideous litany of all the other sorrows.

The mood of our time is that of the end of the world: from armed conflicts to natural disasters, everything seems to demand the suspension of travel and a corresponding retreat into small communities while we wait for the curtain to fall. It would be absurd to deny these real problems, but the only response we ever find for them is fear and reclusion. The words spoken in Davos in 2019 by today's main purveyor of collective panic, Greta Thunberg, are revealing in this respect: "I don't want your hope. I don't want you to be hopeful. I want you to panic. I want you to feel the fear I feel every day."[1] The doctrinaires of Decline and Apocalypse would like to immobilize us with fear so as to keep us at home and capture the ears of the younger generations. Whether the diagnosis is correct or not is irrelevant; what matters is that this is the symptom of a state of mind that preceded the event that confirmed it. As for the post-pandemic world, it will be – it already is – the world of the interior: this is the likely legacy of this mischievous virus that keeps fading away, only to come back again and again. It is as inevitable as the blade of a guillotine: every relaxation of safety measures since the start of the pandemic has immediately been followed by a new outbreak, a new wave of infections, which in turn generates more coercive measures. The interior: this is the negative romance of our time, the prestige of the maternal dwelling, the house as cradle, the home as a womb. Covid was merely a midwife to the actual virus: a pre-existing allergy to the Outside. For three years now, we've experienced an incoherent horror that is at once terrifying and feeble. And what have we learned from it? To wash our hands. This no doubt immense progress doesn't exactly make for a thrilling future.

CHAPTER 2

The Bankruptcy of Eros?

Forty years ago, AIDS imposed an important constraint upon us: that of protecting ourselves in order not to be contaminated. Saliva – a blissful flow whose mixing symbolized that of bodies – was exempt from its curse. Condoms allowed for union without contagion, and this elementary precaution saved several generations. Covid is entirely different: the virus floats in the air and lands on you at random. Perhaps your spouse happened upon it as he crossed paths with a panting jogger, or with a supermarket shopper who exhaled the fatal particles in his vicinity. And so the cycle begins, along with its curse: the whole world hangs on the verdict of a nasal swab. For the Greeks, *pneuma* was the divine breath that generates life, the primordial respiration that later became the Christian Holy Spirit. Now, however, this breath is potentially lethal: its warm moistness can kill. Smelling the other used to be a vertiginous experience; it has now become a sentence. Is there anything more conducive to stopping human warmth in its tracks? The entire ordeal has revealed to us just how happy we were without realizing it, how extraordinary the world's ordinariness used to be.

We have lost the innocence of the common cold, the traditional winter chill that spares no one. At the slightest clearing of the throat or runny nose, we're plagued by doubts: what if it's something more serious? Anyone who coughs near you is a leper who must be urgently driven away.

Will this lead us to develop an eroticism of distance, a "Corona Sutra" with positions recommended by medical professionals? Faced with the dearth of actual skin, will we experience our enjoyment through screens, as in Roger Vadim's 1968 film *Barbarella*, that fantastic B-movie whose heroine, played by Jane Fonda, makes love with her fingertips? These days, we're titillated when someone we desire takes off his mask, as if it were the first step in a full striptease; the only risk is that the unveiled face will disappoint the aspirants who dreamed of being magnetized by a gaze, by the purity of a face. Public life has gone from being the place of human exchange and commerce to that of suspicion. It's a short distance from the caution required of us (vaccinations, health passports, washing) to the destruction of our bonds. Covid has resurrected the two great modern phobias: paranoia, the fear of the other; and hypochondria, the fear of the self – the certainty that our body carries within it the germ or the disease that will kill it.

Certain cultures are able to adapt to this increasing prudishness where contact is concerned. Asians greet one another by bowing and joining their hands: living in great numbers has become second nature for them; they possess an art of living together that is not simply the conformity of the herd, as it is for us. These oceans of humanity that swell and contract have a meaning, a logic, almost a delicateness. North Americans, on the other hand, greet each other so as to better avoid one another. Rather than smiling at you to begin a conversation, they ask you to stay in your place. "I've registered your presence," they seem to say; "now take note of my existence and move on." Just try to be a good Frenchman and kiss a woman you are introduced to – she'll shrink away as though she'd been kissed by a toad, and only the excuse of cultural exoticism will keep her from complaining. The famous "hug" is not a warm embrace but a sort of clutching from a distance that must be performed with your belly tucked in so as to avoid any bodily contact. In France, we traditionally kiss each other on the cheeks, but it is true that this is disappearing, to the great relief of those who can no longer stand this humid gushing, those lips that smack two, three, or four times. It will survive only within the family or among close friends, a forgotten treasure to be registered as a UNESCO cultural heritage. The winners in all of this are the misanthropes, the puritans of every realm.

But what is life worth in the Latin or Mediterranean world if we can't touch each other or hold each other in our arms? We live in Europe, in an urban civilization, and the art of the city is the art par excellence of the theatre – the art of putting on a performance and enjoying the performances of others. Looking at and evaluating yourself is an essential aspect of public life. Few pastimes are more delightful than watching people walk past from the terrace of a café. On this great stage where people of all types, ethnicities, and ages come together, a play is performed that is always the same and yet always different, whose energy fascinates us and wears us out. The crowd surprises itself by way of those who compose it. What will become of this urban enchantment if, at the slightest warning, we have to return to hand coverings, visors, surgical gloves? What will become of the city's physiognomy if it is populated by faceless inhabitants, dressed up like extras in a low-budget medical series? It's like a costume ball whose theme is "outdoor hospital ward." Traditionally, wearing a mask was a game played with others in balls and carnivals. For the last few years – and even though they're becoming rarer – we've used them to swaddle our mouths, as if they had become obscene organs. Today it's the naked face that creates a rift with the "mask people," bursting forth like something vulgar. What? You're still showing your own face? In the middle of the twentieth century, the body was bared, and now it's covered back up; 30 years ago, we had condoms, and today we have masks, gloves, visors, gowns, gowns that go over the gowns, and hygienic caps – not to mention the veils and burkinis that were already here.

But there's more. A previous stage in evolution had already prepared our minds to condemn sensual pleasure: for a long time now, the so-called "stronger" sex has become the suspect sex, and we've arrived at a situation in which "a disturbing presumption of guilt is too often accepted in the realm of sexual offenses,"[1] per the terms of a petition signed by more than a hundred criminal lawyers, all self-proclaimed feminists, reminding us of the principles of the presumption of innocence and the statute of limitations. Should we be surprised that the birth rate collapsed in 2020 (it has since recovered slightly), and that our romantic desires have declined, when mere skin contact is both liable to prosecution, in the event of litigation, and fraught with serious threats to health? The liberation of women's speech is a healthy development. But eroticism entered into an era of defiance when sanitary constraints crossed paths with the injunctions of #MeToo – especially male desire, which was already a priori negative, assumed to be violent and aggressive. If every man is guilty through his natural condition of having a penis, if every boy must be not educated but re-educated to atone for this fundamental flaw, and if every young girl must be persuaded that all amorous encounters between heterosexuals are potential rapes, then how can we be surprised if younger generations are turning to abstinence or chastity?

If François Truffaut's 1968 film *Stolen Kisses* were made today, it would be called *Attempted Harassment*. An elevator taken in the company of a lone woman, a hand that grazes a back, or a simple insistent glance (what in the United States is called a "rape look") can already be considered offensive. Combating sexual assault is legitimate, but making people feel guilty for minor gestures of seduction or pleasure simply leads them to feel obstructed or inhibited. And let's not forget that teenagers today are completely in the grasp of pornography – that imperious schoolteacher who, by way of her unappeasable choreography, devalues the clumsy attempts of beginners and limits them to onanism. The language of love today is entirely dominated by a bellicose boasting: sexual pleasure is experienced not with someone, but only against – men, the patriarchy, capitalism, a rival school of thought. Enjoyment is a weapon pointed at the world, not a moment of delight shared with a fellow being. For the last half-century, the erotic sphere has been structured as a sectarian sphere: even the famous alphabet soup – LGBTQI+++ – has become a battlefield of all against all (gays against lesbians, lesbians against trans . . .), complete with trials, anathemas, and death threats. Libertinism today is a honey spoiled by bitterness: the cult of the body is now adorned with the hideous mask of dogmatism. The inquisitors of the libido are legion, whatever their creed or allegiance. In the 1960s, we used to say "make love, not war," but making love today means triggering the war of all against all. The idea that joy can arise from skin meeting skin has vanished. Sex is no longer a pleasurable activity but a club with which to beat others. This is why the real tendency of our time is less the disorder of the senses than their pure and simple bankruptcy.[2] Will we witness the growth of two new figures, the voluntary virgin and the militant eunuch – proselytes of active abstention, of non-sexuality? This is the strange outcome of a revolution that sought to enflame us, but ended in a bitterness and disenchantment that threatens to destroy our capacity to understand the wonders of the flesh. Eros remains the power of life that connects what is separate, the only universal language that we all speak, a dazzling short-circuit that launches bodies against each other.

The relations between the two sides of humanity have not improved – they have become more complex: emancipation is not the same as serenity. But if they are not easier, at least they are more interesting, since they now set beings of (almost) equal strength face to face with each other. It is not certain that men and women can be reconciled, and live in harmony around a few republican principles, solely by dint of concessions and laws: the division of labor, anatomical destiny, and professional inequalities will forever hinder an idyllic harmony. Sexism, even if punishable by law, will not disappear: each sex remains, for its unfathomable opposite, neither so different nor so near as it thinks; each is a source of fear and wonder for the other. And as a result, every relationship is wrapped up in ambiguity, in the indistinguishable sharing out of attraction and fear. Just like in past times, relationships between men and women today are woven with commonplaces that are no sooner denied than confirmed, and that form the basis of both their mutual animosity and their mutual attraction. We will never see the end of discord between the sexes (or between majorities and minorities, for that matter), but it is up to us to bring it away from the fanatics of both sides, and their perpetual belligerence. Regardless of mutual deafness, regardless of disappointment, we must preserve at all costs this atmosphere of erotic and loving friendship that makes the Europe of today a place of highly developed civilization.

Today's abandonment of sex is the symptom of an allergy to others. The real tragedy would be to one day cease to love and desire, which would lead this magical two-sided fount – our very attachment to existence – to dry up. The opposite of libido is not abstinence, but the fatigue of living.

CHAPTER 3

Forbidden Travel?

"Man's unhappiness arises from one thing alone: that he cannot remain quietly in his room," writes Pascal. And he continues: "That is why men so love noise and activity. That is why jail is such a horrible punishment. That is why the pleasure of solitude is incomprehensible."[1] We might retort that all of man's misfortune in the years to come may derive from not wanting to leave his room. What will threaten him then will be less the virus than inaction, less the risk of falling sick than perishing of boredom. With all due respect to Pascal, entertainment is essential, futile pursuits are vital, travel is indispensable, and without these intermissions that interrupt our daily routines, existence would quickly come to resemble penitence. Between his meditation on the misery of the man without God and the one dealing with distraction, there is a third term that Pascal, a man of the *Ancien Régime*, could not perceive: action and work.

There are two words that characterize our current situation: *Obstruction* and *Complication*. Why make it simple when you can make it complicated? What used to be easy has become complex, and what used to be difficult has become almost impossible. Until recently, drinking a coffee at the bar or on the terrace of a café required a pass; buying a baguette meant wearing a mask; and going shopping meant waiting in long queues, like in the cold war-era USSR. Going abroad still entails a mountain of obstacles if you don't have everything in order, and let's not even mention getting a passport. The stream of travelers is subject to drastic conditions that keep getting worse. The sheer breadth of what is prohibited has grown in inconceivable ways, and it is hard to see how we can go back. Let's not forget the online forms, the receipts, the still-mandatory tests, the countless QR codes. Covid will be remembered as one more step in the increased control of people's daily lives and movements. Someone always finds fault in whatever we do. Since the outbreak of the pandemic, France has displayed a genius worthy of Courteline in building a bureaucratic maze of prohibitions, restrictions, limitations, and optional constraints, all with a lexical richness – a capacity for inventing jargon – that linguists will delight in. It was not the only country to succumb to this madness: few nations have escaped the pandemic's administrative nightmare; China in particular has brought it to a unique level of abomination. We have not fallen into dictatorship, as some misguided minds have been quick to proclaim; we have simply suffered the bumps of a messy improvisation, and in this regard, democracies, in spite of everything, have proven their flexibility and their superiority over autocracies. But it is now clear that people are willing to sacrifice certain freedoms for the sake of safety. There is only one reasonable way out of this situation: staying at home. There will never be a shortage of reasons to ask men and women to dig little holes for themselves, all under the benevolent watch of the State: the plagues of Egypt have descended upon a humanity that is all too fearful in the North, and all too destitute in the South. Opening the door will become a highly perilous act, in conformity with the ambiguity of the lock, which one turns to enter the home after a busy day, but which one also turns to keep the outside from entering. The excessive enlargement of domestic space is a reaction to the shrinking of public space. This demands that we limit our possessions, our ambitions, our movements: the man of the future is a reduced being who corresponds perfectly to the augmented reality of the virtual. More and more, to exist means to withdraw. The first lockdown had the advantage of novelty: it was almost picturesque in its brutality. It promised to be brief. The following ones came to seem like a self-fulfilling prophecy. What if they become the face of our future, if they shape the world of tomorrow – a world of stifled speech, distancing, distrust, and increased regulations? Over the last few years, we've become like "Plato in a dressing gown" (as Levinas said of Oblomov), holding forth on the effectiveness of vaccines, the "conspiracy" of big pharma, the lies of our leaders, the dangers of collective existence. There is a sweetness to our internment and even a pleasure in our confined existence that are reminiscent, as we'll see below, of the long tradition of Western monasticism: think of the monk's cell and of social networks. The pleasure we associate with our shells is adorned with all the virtues of resistance – to climate change, insecurity, and the world's perils. *Indoor life instead of inner life.* It is now imperative for us to maintain this plant-like immobility so as not to expose ourselves or produce an outsized carbon footprint. The Earth has once more become immense – in other words, forbidden. The world is closing in on itself: hitchhiking across the globe with a backpack has become a utopian dream. The lockdown entailed a shrinking of space, a distension of time; now that it is over, the opposite has occurred: distances have increased exponentially. Crossing borders is once more a feat, a grueling handicap race. The near has become far – and the far, inaccessible.

Take the *flygskam* ("flight shame") popularized by environmental activists in Sweden: we should stop using planes to avoid adding to our greenhouse gas debt. But according to the International Civil Aviation Organization, the aviation sector accounts for only 3 percent of global emissions. No matter – some are motivated by the desire not to fight against global warming but to punish the human species. We need to nail it to the ground, they suggest, to teach it a good lesson. Instead of proposing concrete goals to citizens, planting trees by the millions, restoring desertified soil, making homes more energy efficient, and gradually learning to do without fossil fuels that enrich dictatorships (Russia, Qatar, Saudi Arabia, Algeria), they are content to heap opprobrium on those who resist them, seeking to make them feel guilty. Changing our lives now means reducing them as much as possible. Every era is a field on which opposing tendencies lock horns, but there are many today who would like to block this field's horizon, and convert us to a troglodyte morality. It is one thing to advocate a policy of sobriety, quite another to discourage travel or criminalize cars. Many within the environmental movement are already warning against a return to traditional tourism, which they view as an aberration drowning in its own success. Didn't the Green Party mayor of Poitiers, Léonore Moncond'huy, decide in April of 2021, for the benefit of the planet, to cut subsidies to the association Rêves de gosse – "Childhood Dreams" – which allows disabled children to fly for the first time? According to her, "flying should no longer be part of children's dreams."[2] Please remain at ground level at all times. We're witnessing a reappraisal of cars, planes, trucks, cruise ships, tankers, and – in Paris – scooters and motorcycles. *The new nationalist or climatic narrative always tries to appeal to our innermost being.* Within this melancholy context, all that remains is to take stock of what is forbidden to us in the name of the planet, health, or the defense of borders that now bristle with moats, spike strips, and machicolations. Freedom has become a burden from which only enclosure delivers us.

Our sleepy citizens are told to stay in bed – *in other words, to lie down, all the better to be submissive.* The slightest infraction or excess, we are told, will increase our carbon footprint, further wounding the planet and delaying its healing. Hence the idea of setting individual consumption quotas to limit pollution. A new aristocracy of the "carbon-sober" will now form the elite, whom the majority will have to imitate. Didn't a commentator on public radio recently explain that men and women, in order to seduce each other, should show off their low carbon footprints instead of nice cars or expensive jewellery? There's nothing like a climate passport to melt people's hearts. We'll all soon have our own "ecometers" – ecological thermometers that will measure our daily debts. In France, there's a new game for children to raise awareness about respecting the planet, called the "Zero Waste Family." This is no doubt a magnificent initiative. But will a saga consisting of peelings and the sorting of garbage really replace Cluedo or Trivial Pursuit in our children's imagination? If, as Tennessee Williams wrote, "desire is something that is made to occupy a larger space than that which is afforded by the individual being,"[3] then what remains of desire when it is put on a weight-loss program? Nations, individuals, and families have all been won over by *a fragmentation complex*, which consists of reducing the space we occupy to an extreme, and results in each of us being wedged into our own niche. The transfixed crowds who march for the climate, in a way reminiscent of flagellants in the Middle Ages, do so as victims seeking to make amends rather than as political actors. They wail, scream, and cry, depriving themselves of their own agency as they protest. For a generation raised with the prospect of coming disaster, fed on the milk of terror, and persuaded of being History's unloved ones, it's not difficult to imagine that any exit from the cocoon might come to seem like a considerable expenditure of energy.

It is also possible that, with the spread of working from home and state hand-outs almost from birth, we will see, in the near future, a reduction in life's labors: *The Right to Be Lazy*, originally a book written at the end of the nineteenth century by Paul Lafargue (son-in-law of Karl Marx), a panegyric on consumer society and compulsory entertainment before either existed, will quite simply become a reality for most. With a double consequence: a large part of the population, helpless and idle, will have to be entertained day and night – hypnotized before their screens, they'll plunge into the nightmare of inescapable leisure. Activity, that great calming influence on modern souls, will become the luxury of the privileged, and idleness the burden of the poor. This is a reversal of the ancient curse attached to labor: the very rich will work outrageous hours, taking pride in their exhaustion, while everyone else will claim benefits, living on assistance and a guaranteed minimum income. Work could soon become (at least in France, where salaries are very low) a rare commodity reserved for the wealthy, while the plebs will be entertained to their heart's content – the pandemic has merely accelerated this trend. Aren't we already seeing a predominance of "homewear," at the expense of office attire, in all but high-end clothing? And remote work, by dispersing both employees and executives to every corner of the country, will have a nefarious effect on firms and offices, which, whatever their shortcomings, were hives of activity that allowed people to make contacts and develop bonds.

It is a symptom of our time that we no longer speak of change but of salvation: we must save the planet, save France, save Europe, save the polar bears, save the left or the right. Thinking in such absolute dichotomies makes partial measures seem piddling: total solutions or death! But in order to preserve – a landscape, an area, a language, a country – sometimes we have to innovate and disrupt. Human life was once a passage from birth to death, a simple pilgrimage. Now we live in constant transition: from childhood to maturity, from fossil fuels to renewable energies, and from sex at birth to chosen gender, transition is as natural for us as breathing. But what's our destination? In the end, evolving from one state to another, calling oneself fluid or non-binary, becomes an identity – in other words, yet another confinement. Freedom is a quality that can be learned, but it can also be unlearned, and a single generation suffices to dispel our appetite for it. Freedom means the possibility of creating something new on this earth and the ability of each person to lead his life as he wishes – to feel unique. Covid has not only killed millions of people, disrupted the entire planet, impoverished the middle classes, destroyed friendships, divided couples, fostered marital violence, produced an explosion of obesity and a proliferation of pets (especially dogs), it has also freed us from freedom as an ideal. And since the only tomorrows we can imagine are undesirable, let's use today to slow down: let's allow our urges to subside and chain the Dionysian horde of our desires. Let's become truly still waters that nothing can awaken.

The great stage on which we act out our lives is now the sofa or the couch – in front of a screen, of course, the only bulwark against the world's horrors, which arrive filtered by images, reinforcing our desire to stay at home. From

Los Angeles to Beijing, this is the setting in which all of humanity moves about today. Each in his own dwelling – in his own house, apartment, garden, yurt, bunker. The lockdown has reduced us to the size of our living rooms; prohibited from going beyond this perimeter, our only movement is that of our eyes following flows of information. Our pyjamas have become "political objects," per the claim of Jean-Claude Kaufmann,[4] like a stone in the hand of a rioter, or a voting ballot in the hand of a citizen. We resist the attacks of the cruel world in our dressing gowns and slippers. But our slippers are connected to our computers, our iPads, our smartphones, and the entire planetary Web: they are cosmic, interstellar. Is this really enough for us? What satisfaction can it give us, other than that of feeling like a swordfish in a bathtub (as Alain Souchon has said), with no recourse but to change the bathwater?

We've taken off our masks, but we have perhaps been gagged in the process. Here we are, under existential house arrest, as a result of only the best intentions. What some have called health-related tyranny has been replaced by a *tyranny of sedentariness*. Don't move: keep as still as a statue. Given this, it's not surprising that the main opposition to health measures on both sides of the Atlantic has come from people who drive for a living, whether in cars or trucks; indeed, this was already the case with the *gilets jaunes* in France in 2018. A new anthropological type is emerging: the shriveled, hyperconnected being who no longer needs others or the outside world. All of today's technologies encourage incarceration under the guise of openness. And how can we fail to understand the desire to stay home and work remotely by those who for years have endured the hell of commuting, office life, and being micromanaged by their bosses? We should rephrase Rimbaud's famous line "Real life is absent"[5] as follows:

"Real life is the absence of life." For all those who still extoll the virtues of exploration, of being around others, this is insult added to injury: in addition to the 18 to 20 million deaths worldwide, the penance of stunting in the guise of atonement.

In the past, we thought the belief in reason would allow us to master nature and the globe itself. *From the Closed World to the Infinite Universe*, per the title of the historian Alexandre Koyré's 1957 book – we went from the closed cosmos of the Middle Ages to the expansive one of the Renaissance. Five centuries later, we are experiencing the opposite: our knowledge and technologies seem unlimited, but we encounter one border after another the moment we step outside. Each of us, bombarded with distressing information, whether alone or with his family, in his bedroom or his living room, views the land of the Outside as a place where danger reigns. But the land of the Inside is not exempt from dangers either: it delivers us to the powers of solitude, banality, inexorable boredom, the fatigue of being, the fog of the soul. Everything, or almost everything, has become possible at home: home catering, entertainment, cinema, concerts, and theatre, all accessible thanks to subscriptions and platforms; online workouts with personal trainers; remote work and video games; occasional sex through Tinder or Grindr. You can even have safe sex with remote partners, using sensors and vibrators. It's the reign of the "just like" – just like a restaurant, a gym, a date . . . But isn't it, in reality, just like nothing?

CHAPTER 4

Is a Banal Life Worth Living?

"Everyday life" hasn't always existed; behind its seeming simplicity lies an enigma. It was Flemish painting in the seventeenth century that probably marked the birth and apogee of this notion. This school's predilection for interior subjects – a woman in the kitchen, a man writing a letter, a mother breastfeeding her child, sleeping soldiers, a reader immersed in her book – marked a real turning point: it established a prosaicness that had until then been masked by religious paintings or battle scenes featuring only saints or heroes. The great novelty, as Tzvetan Todorov has noted,[1] is that ordinary people were suddenly worthy of representation. Didn't Hegel explain that the genius of Protestantism was to bind the faithful to the ordinariness of life? On the outside, disorder; on the inside, peace, gentleness, and the graceful unfolding of human passions. There is nothing trivial about these paintings: the things they show are good because they exist. Bourgeois, peasants, craftsmen, soldiers, prostitutes: all are worthy of interest in their own right. It's a revolution that is both pictorial and mental, *elevating the trivial and belittling the noble*. The humblest activities – peeling turnips, playing the flute, repairing a piece of furniture, combing one's hair in a mirror – have no less value than the coronation of a monarch or the deeds of classical heroes. The glorification of the familiar forms the framework in which every human being flourishes with his loved ones: there is a joy in being at home, and domestic values deserve praise. Both truculent and ambiguous, the everyday world comes into its own in the light shed by art. It is the revenge of the common man on exceptional beings. This early realism manifested what Eugène Fromentin would later call a "tenderness for the real" that was never repeated. It is the great epiphany of the mundane as a place of human flourishing. For a time, the curse on the sensible world was lifted.

Everyday life did not retain this impression of freshness for long. In the centuries that followed, it became as much an object of rejection as of fascination. The naturalist school of the French novel, with all its meticulous documentation, took pleasure in darkness: from Zola to Huysmans, to describe was always more or less to condemn or disparage, to manifest a taste for sordid details. In the 1960s, Duane Hanson, an American artist who has now been largely forgotten, scored a huge success by creating sculptures of ordinary citizens in fiberglass and resin, which he then displayed in public spaces: supermarket cashiers, vacationers in Bermuda shorts, people mowing the lawn, or couples out on the town, all reproduced with mind-boggling precision. Anyone walking down the street or in a park could come across his double and be tempted to greet him. Claiming to be a hyper-realist, Duane Hanson created a veritable Grévin Museum of the average American, whose symbol is the *Supermarket Lady*, a housewife wearing curlers and slippers and pushing her cart through a shopping mall. In this exhaustive repertory of human types, the models' proximity to real people was unsettling and almost frightening. These beings resemble us, and, like us, they are perfectly interchangeable. Their inexpressive eyes seem to come from another planet. They are all imbued with an irrepressible melancholy that affects their every gesture, and bears witness to an abysmal emptiness. These anonymous figures could be anyone: you, me, your neighbor, any man or woman. (It is one of the hallmarks of the Grévin Museum to freeze stars in wax as though in an ice floe, the better to melt them into a museified anonymity.) The simulacrum has become a grimace.

The classical Christian universe opposed the profane to the sacred, the earthly city to the celestial city. The modern world pits platitude against plenitude: the beyond no longer reigns over the terrestrial realm. Life turned ordinary once we became children of the calendar and the payroll, once our existence was broken down into weeks, months, and pay slips. Every century has its banal aspects, but modernity, by cutting itself off from transcendence, has truly brought it to light. The world was once oriented: existence, consigned to brevity, was obsessed with the salvation of the soul, which would redeem original sin. Death was not an end point, but a door that opened onto an unknown world, whether of abomination or of bliss. From the Renaissance onward, concern for happiness gradually replaced anxiety about eternity. Fleeting pleasures, condemned by Christian moralists such as Bossuet and Pascal, found unprecedented favor, especially as advances in medicine and agriculture lengthened life expectancy. And as man replaced God as the foundation of the law during the French Revolution, daily life gained a certain autonomy. Its meaning is no longer written in advance. We have a degree of freedom to innovate: it depends on us, and us alone, to give direction to our lives.[2] And thus, life can improvise, but it can also engage in repetition, limiting itself to endlessly doing the same things. Sometimes our days, which are all alike, begin to stutter. It is thus that banality is born – this disease of a time that doesn't move in any particular direction and repeats itself with the constancy of a broken record. This repetition comes with a price and takes an exorbitant toll on us: it bores us and at the same time exhausts us. Our life is all the more wearying in that nothing happens in it. The mystery of this phenomenon is that it wears us out with its inconsistency. The more things return, identical to themselves, the more they overwhelm us. Each day is a replica of the previous one and an anticipation of the next one, which is a perfect description of stress – the microscopic war of attrition made up of annoyances and minor worries. "When you live," writes Sartre in *Nausea*, "nothing happens. Settings change, people come and go, and that's it. There are no beginnings. Days are added to days without rhyme or reason, in an interminable and monotonous addition."

From this endless rehashing arises a very modern form of fatigue, one without grandeur, and that derives not from extraordinary feats but from the eternal return of the same occurrences. If regularity is the condition for fruitful work and long-term projects, it is also a fog in which we lose our way. We're somehow exhausted from doing nothing, subjected to an aggression all the more violent for appearing calm. Life is at once pacified and a constant battle. Little worries, little anxieties, rushing here and there: it all amounts to nothing in the end, but it still seems like too much. Add to this the fatigue of being oneself,[3] born of the obligation to behave as a free and liberated subject. The most ordinary life is still too hectic, exhausting us with its demands and disappointing us with its monotony. The tedious is not only tedious, it's exhausting. Everyday life is unique in that it neutralizes everything, abolishes contrasts and drowns love, anger, passions, and hopes in a kind of undifferentiated haze. Since the nineteenth century, a certain type of literature has been lamenting the same thing: a cyclical life that is both uniform and harsh, and that stupefies us as much as it wears us out. This is the phenomenon that forms the framework of our modernity. A life without significant events is not a neutral life: the passing of time, the time that simply unfolds, hour after hour, takes its toll on us – it demolishes us without our even realizing it. Living has a cost. Even inertia is still tension and aggression.

It would be nice if we could elevate this slow corrosion, this insidious war with our nerves, to the level of tragedy. Yet it is not a destiny, just a succession of twists and turns that are of no interest to anyone. And the abstract fatigue that results is itself of a very special nature, the fruit not of hyperactivity but of routine. Nothing happens, but this nothing is almost the same as an attack, and absorbs as much energy as a thrilling adventure. The world is moving too fast, as they say, and the digitization of even the simplest services is a perfect example. Instead of simplifying everything, it has made things more complex, with the same result. Especially as the world is going nowhere, which means that this acceleration makes no sense. Like the Red Queen in *Through the Looking-Glass*, we're forced to run about just to stay where we are. Inertia causes irreparable damage: it's an erosion that attacks our moods and our energy. "These things only happen to me, says the man to whom nothing happens" (Jacques Prévert). Everyday life lacks the appeal of fiction, which is suspense. The same events recur with dreadful predictability, and everything is rehashed ad infinitum. The question "What's new?" always elicits the same answer: "Nothing much." Something is always starting up again without anything really having begun. This is forcefully expressed in certain paintings by Edward Hopper, who depicted urban landscapes as places in suspension: a woman at her window looking down at the street,[4] waiting for who knows what; anonymous people in the windows of a café, slightly stooped, despairing of unlikely changes.

Exhaustion and overwork make up our modern lives, as Nietzsche put it. In a constant battle with ghosts – in other words, with downtime – we have been critically wounded by dullness: it takes such a great concentration of energy just to keep our daily lives going at an acceptable level. We have all the drawbacks of fragmentation without any of the benefits of real diversion, and the way our fortunes seem to sink without ever rising comes to appear, simply, as everyday life. A sentimental Buddhism has arisen, promoted by hordes of life coaches, who propose Zen, meditation, and simply letting go, to give our monotonous existence a spiritual crutch. The liberated and the peaceful put themselves forth as models of serenity. And they have every right to do so – but they slow down a pace that is already torpid. What we need to combat stress isn't calm but an actual event – an escape from ourselves. The simple anxiety of being, this tension without intensity, gives rise to an irrepressible need for painkillers and rest. Relaxation is the remedy for low-key lives whose tiny fluctuations are still too exuberant for those who experience them. The acceleration of time gives an illusory feeling of fullness – in fact, this whirlwind produces nothing but emptiness, as its myriad temptations don't even make a dent in our routines. This is the strange feeling that rules the modern age: at the heart of our numbed existences, we feel like we're caught in a gust of wind that we must do everything in our power to resist. Faced with colorless days, we erect barriers of tranquility; we search out prescriptions and psychotropic drugs instead of testing ourselves with strong activity and powerful emotions. What we need is not wisdom but a sort of gentle madness – not a spiritual balm but an intoxication. This is what the lockdown made clear by forcibly plunging us into a grueling prosaicness, thus giving rise to a dull anxiety through the obligation to do nothing. Living, as Paul Valéry said, is an essentially monotonous practice based on predictability and repetition. But repetition scatters us at the same time as it calms us: a perfect entropy.

In the past, the great religious question was: Is there life after death? The great question of secular societies is the opposite: Have we lived enough before death? Have we loved enough, given enough, lavished enough, embraced enough? Existence is not an endurance race in which we have to hold out as long as possible against life's blows, but a certain quality of bonds, emotions, and commitments. When it is reduced to withdrawing into a shell, to staring at a screen to play video games, binge series, or engage in compulsive shopping, does it still have the slightest value? Whether we want to slow down time or speed it up, protect ourselves from danger or expose ourselves to it, we need to feel things that move us, that belong to the realm of grace. To experience the shock of change, we need to begin by breaking with the torpor of identical days so as to feel the revelatory power of the new – something that a life spent locked away does not allow.

CHAPTER 5

The Bovarysme of the Cell Phone

If remorse, for Baudelaire, is the impossibility of undoing a crime or a transgression, banality, conversely, is the powerlessness to do, to inaugurate something new, to open a breach in the mass of hours that all come to resemble one another. Didn't Levinas write of Oblomov that laziness is "an impossibility of beginning"; didn't Oblomov himself say he was too lazy to live? What he needed was the heroism that consists in getting up: the mad courage to get out of bed to welcome a new day, to set his feet down on the ground, to throw off the blanket, to face the century – all of which he lacked. The housebound world of everyday life is not lacking in seduction for those willing to let themselves be carried along by the passage from morning to afternoon and from afternoon to evening. It's a sedative pleasure, where you operate in a quasi-automatic mode, and it's the experience – appalling for some, delectable for others – that billions of earthlings lived through between 2020 and 2022.

The word "laziness" has two meanings: the ordinary one, an aversion to labor, and the more metaphysical one, that of being overwhelmed by existence conceived of "as a burden" (Levinas).[1] The former is a refusal to waste living by earning one, while the latter is an abdication, a radical impossibility of being. Since living weighs you down, curling up in your cocoon is a way of avoiding this burden – at the risk of neutralizing all appetite and all desire. This is the ambivalence of our domestic Guantánamos: we cherish them until the moment they turn against us, strangling us like an octopus's embrace. The drowsiness of our perpetual Sabbath eventually becomes a form of oppression. The invention of the cell phone at the end of the twentieth century was a truly brilliant response to this. Not only does it connect us to everyone at any time of day or night (hence making it unacceptable not to answer immediately) – the uniqueness of this tiny box lies in the fact that it eludes what it offers us. It brings the world (messages, news, music, films) into our homes, which is undeniably an enormous advancement, but it also makes the world superfluous, since I have it in the palm of my hand. It comes to me, and I no longer need to go to it. The cell phone also makes the world useless, because its potential will always exceed anything that could actually happen to me. This planetary agora enables us to speak to each other across continents without any need to travel. If we check it hundreds of times a day, like a Bible or an electronic missal, it's not to draw advice or moral teachings from it, but because it offers us a hectic existence whose experience it spares us. We feel it in our pockets, in our palms, to be sure of being alive, connected to everyone.

There's always something happening on my smartphone: it's bursting with interesting news, surprises, games, and apps, and it seems to be the only thing that can spice up a dull day with something new. But it's less a spice than a perpetual distraction. This jingling little animal is a veritable electronic lasso, summoning me to its bedside at the slightest whimper and prompting me to respond at every turn. Expecting everything from a miniature jewel box means giving up on life in favor of a tool to which we delegate our desires and passions. It should be a simple machine, but we're the ones who are at its service. We try detox cures, we turn it off for the whole day, we put it in a basket during work meetings, we willfully forget about it – and the excitement of reuniting with it is like finding a lost love. What we expect from it belongs to the logic of universal Bovarysme: mad hope followed by abysmal disappointment. We want it to provoke or announce an earth-shattering event. The fact that we can be instantly connected with a loved one, wherever he may be, makes waiting and the experience of non-reciprocity intolerable. Why doesn't he – she – call me? We fall back on the little god of technological accidents – a dead battery, a weak signal, a theft – but the reality is crueler: the other person simply doesn't want to talk to you.

"Mobile, dear mobile, tell me something wonderful is going to happen to me. Surprise me, surprise me," exclaim the millions of users who consult it at all hours of the day and night, in the subway, on the bus, on the train, on the plane, all of them addicted to it, compelled at the slightest tremor to run toward it. The most beautiful cell phone can't give you anything more than what it is, a sophisticated communications system; it can't create friends, lovers, a future. It's so sad to see so many helots on trains, buses, and planes spending their time on their phones, playing games and watching series instead of talking to others, admiring the scenery, or opening a book to escape, to delve into the twists and turns of the past, to expand their horizons. The very fact of its plethora, its excess, renders the screen empty. And the addiction it produces stems from the fact that, with it, events are not experienced but received, by proxy. When nothing is happening in life, at least the phone is there to forge a simulacrum of reality.

What it will always fail to give us is the firm consistency of actual developments, real turns of events. In an uncertain world, it offers the thrill without the peril, and allows us to endure emptiness. But this exuberance is an illusion. For a large segment of humanity, the cell phone has become a new organ that will probably soon be grafted to our ears and eyes like a prosthesis. The digital age marks the triumph of distraction and the defeat of attention.[2] We've relinquished self-control to engage in a constant search for new forms of gratification; this frenetic manipulation is matched only by the poverty of our experience. How many of us can't share a meal or a conversation with a friend or spouse without feverishly consulting our device? It orders us to respond immediately to messages or face the consequences. It diverts us from everything, including ourselves, in a frantic flight to the next text message, the next call. This tool of communication with others prevents us from conversing with those closest to us, except in a fragmented and discontinuous way. We constantly have to deal with intruders in buses, trains, stores, who speak loudly into their phones, shamelessly letting you into their intimacy. The new prosthetic man or woman is constantly whipping out their phones, looking for urgent news, even during lovemaking, like a warrior unsheathing his sword on the front line: could it be that they've missed a call, a text, an alert? In English, and also in Frenglish, one calls this phenomenon FOMO: the fear of missing out. When we're on our phones, we fall in love with the latest occurrence, the latest enticement; their avalanche, indeed their explosion, is even more exciting than finding out about potential partners.

We may soon see the spread of withdrawal hotels, where guests will pay dearly to have their laptops and computers confiscated for days at a time, sleep in rooms with no television or radio, and be connected to the world by nothing more than an old-fashioned landline telephone, its receiver jingling on its stand. All they'll have at their disposal, if they so desire, is old-fashioned paper newspapers and old-fashioned hardback books; they'll have to talk face to face and touch each other like they did in the old days. They'll pretend they're in the past as a kind of therapy, so as to be able to cope with the present.

CHAPTER 6

Cave, Cell, and Bedroom

When he wrote the myth of the cave, Plato set the mental scene that continues to haunt Western consciousness. Men are chained up in a cave, unable to turn their heads, made to face a wall. All they can see are the reflections of a fire lit far behind them, at a certain elevation, and the shadows of other men who pass on a track before the fire. The prisoners take these shadows to be the sole reality, and consider them more real than the light that generates them.[1] If one of these captives were forced to contemplate the light, i.e. the truth, he would be dazzled and "even blinded," and would immediately want to return to the cave and its soothing half-light. Only the boldest and most daring are able to turn away from the illusions of the cave and contemplate the starry sky, the sun, the heavenly bodies. But doing so means they can't go back down among the captives, partake in their errors, and accustom themselves to the darkness once again. For Socrates, who explains this myth to Glaucon, the cave is a representation of the sensible world, which is prey to error, while the sky embodies the intelligible world of the Good and Beautiful. He who passes from divine contemplation to lowly human things will find it hard to converse with coarse beings in the grip of falsity. Socrates deduces from this that the prisoners of the cave need education to be elevated little by little to the knowledge and contemplation of pure Ideas. The chosen few who have seen the True and the Good must go back down among the prisoners to teach them virtue. These chosen ones are the philosophers, who return to the "common abode" to enlighten their fellow citizens. Humanity lives in chiaroscuro, and only philosophy can convert it to the light that is the realm of Being.

This allegory founded European philosophy and its idealism, and continues to interest us for its symbolic richness. How can we fail to see that the myth has been inverted? For in the time since Plato, we've fitted out our caves with all the instruments of modern comfort. We've made of this enclosure not a place of darkness but, on the contrary, one of protection and health. The cave is now the authentic sphere, while the outside world, with its reflections that stream continuously on our screens, attests to violence and savagery. Since the eighteenth century in Europe, private life has become the sanctuary in which modern man constructs himself, enjoys the company of friends and family, and decides on his own destiny. We no longer oppose the world of perishable phenomena to that of immutable essences, but public space to private space. Each era has a different conception of the movement from one to the other, but this back-and-forth dynamic remains fundamental. To live in the world, man must have a shelter in which to take refuge, rest, and protect himself. Immanuel Kant, perhaps because he lived in a time of great insecurity, thought of the home as the sole rampart against the horror of nothingness, as it encloses within its walls all that humanity has patiently gathered over the centuries; that the freedom of man flourishes in stable and enclosed spaces rather than the open and infinite; and that our identity is essentially domiciliary, which is why revolutionaries, who reject hearth and home, condense within themselves all the anguish of wandering.[2]

From across the centuries, Plato sketched out the décor of the modern home: cave plus electricity and social networks. Between ancient Greece and the twenty-first century, another human type emerged: that of the monk in his cell at the dawn of Christianity. What is the aim of a man who has withdrawn from the world – such as Rancé (depicted by Chateaubriand), who voluntarily confined himself to La Trappe Abbey – if not to bear witness to another order within this world? Inaugurated by Theravāda Buddhism 25 centuries ago, monasticism has taken on a particular inflection in Christianity, in both the West and the Middle East. The monastic rule codified by Saint Benedict in the twelfth century, with its division of the day's hours and the long periods it reserves for meditation and prayer, heralds the experience of secular time as we know it today. The monk or nun, in addition to dropping their civil status to take on solely a first name, have the distinctive feature that they are subject, just like us, to that great enigmatic power called daily life, which can lead them toward God or turn them away from Him. It is probably in the muted shadow of monasteries and convents that the West has instilled in itself a meticulous clock-based discipline. What attracts us to monastic life is less austerity than the regularity of an entirely timed existence: placing yourself in God's hands means surrendering to a rigorous set of rules that frees you from the dread of having to manage your time. The "dream life of monks" (Nicolas Diat) lies in the daily recurrence of the same events – a balance between praying, silence, speaking, and working. Fidelity to the Lord is first and foremost fidelity to the times set for meeting Him. The primary function of bells is to indicate the time, with codes and language that differ depending on whether it is midnight or midday, whether what is at stake is a celebration or a funeral toll. The bell is a musical messenger that delivers information and sets the rhythm of time (whether for work or rest) or guides the traveler lost in a storm.[3] There are two ways of living in a retreat from the world: that of the layman who needs a moment to reflect, a brief interlude to meditate; and that of the monk, for whom the monastery is his whole life, interrupted only by work in the fields, or visits to the sick or dying.

Protestants replaced prayer with work, making the latter a quasi-religious act, and accused monks of being parasites who grew fat at the expense of the faithful and sank into licentiousness. God is everywhere, Erasmus said: the entire Christian world is but a single monastery, and all men canons and brothers of a single order.[4] In his own way, the monk is a kind of overworked being – or, at the very least, is constantly kept on his toes by a merciless calendar. Like each of us, when his fervour fades, he too must "endure duration," as Vladimir Jankélévitch once put it – in other words, bear the weight of ordinary time. For as long as he is inhabited by faith, every hour that he can offer to the glory of God and the salvation of his soul is precious. But a fearsome poison sometimes finds its way into monks' hearts: acedia (from the Greek *akēdeia*, meaning indifference or sorrow), that terrible illness that turns ascetics away from the Lord and strikes them with sadness. It is the terrible weariness of the one whom prayer begins to bore even though he has dedicated his life to prayer and adoration, who undergoes a sudden disinterest in his own salvation – a terrible evil against which the Church has proved powerless:

When this passion has taken hold of a monk's soul, it engenders within him a loathing for the place where he

39

lives, a disgust for his cell, and a contempt for the brothers
who live with him or are far away, whom he considers
negligent or unspiritual. It makes him listless and deprives
him of courage for all the work he has to do inside his cell,
preventing him from remaining there and applying himself
to reading [. . .] In the end, he believes he will not be able
to ensure his salvation if he remains in this place, if he does
not leave as soon as possible, abandoning the cell in which
he will have to perish if he remains there.[5]

In these places of retreat in which fervor and contemplation should reign, boredom allows moodiness to enter;
an insidious fog creeps in and corrupts the radiant house,
attacking people's hearts, depleting their energy, and
subjecting the quest for the immutable to the assaults of
the ephemeral.

Whence the need to keep the monk busy day and night,
to divide up his mental space, and to badger him with
diverse tasks as demanding as they are useless, lest the Evil
One enter him and cause his mind to wander. The ascetic,
the cenobite, and the hermit are the first victims of banality.
And, as is the case for us as well, this banality manifests
itself in two seemingly opposed phenomena: an immense
weariness counterbalanced by busyness, and a search
for frenetic rituals, masses, chants, and genuflections.
Because the monk's life is reduced to a long invocation of
the Absent One, because this life is constantly faced with
God's silence, it is more exposed to idleness and to the
miasma of simple duration. The horrified monk whose
direct link with God has been severed observes that his
interiority is suddenly empty. And let us note that monastic
asceticism seems to have become the watchword of the
latest form of capitalism, as in the photograph of Steve
Jobs in his California home, cup of tea in hand, seated on
the floor in an immense empty room furnished only with
a lamp and a record player: we might think of this as an

ostentatious minimalism.[6] At the time, all Apple employees had to follow a strict discipline of frugality and wear the same uniform. The monastery, with its confusion of rule and life, became a blueprint for the factory, the office, the school, the hospital, and the prison – the mold for all of our institutions.

At bottom, interiority is a metaphor. If you go inside yourself to find out what it's like there, all you find is space. In the Christian world, Saint Augustine was the first to describe private space as a site of expropriation: at the heart of the earthly creature lies nothing but darkness, an opacity to which only divine power holds the key. My self is not my own, for in the depths of my being lies absolute otherness, divine transcendence, for which we must hasten to step aside. To seek interiority is to encounter a God "more inward than my most inward part,"[7] the God of the heart. The self is an illusion if it is not homage to the Most High, as later confirmed by Meister Eckhart, Pascal, and Francis de Sales. A millennium later, Rousseau would inflect this diagnosis, saying: "Two almost irreconcilable opposites are united within me,"[8] and hence concluding that nothing is so dissimilar to him as himself; but he attributed this division to the wickedness of the world, to the relentlessness of its slanderers, and not to the greatness of the Lord. From Augustine, inventor of interiority as the greatest distance from self to self, to Rousseau, inventor of intimacy as the expulsion of self by others, more than 13 centuries went by, during which Europe became largely secularized, and earthly life was rehabilitated. But in both cases, the inner self is inhabited by another: for Augustine, the Lord, sacred occupant of my innermost being; for Rousseau, slanderous humanity. Later, psychology, Freudian psychoanalysis, and literature would explore the darkroom of the mind – this box that is sometimes empty, sometimes overcrowded with family members, and utterly indecipherable, for we had lost its code. Boasting of a rich inner life is a privilege enjoyed only by prisoners in the Gulag or Nazi camps, capable of reciting entire poems to their comrades in the cold and terror. To reflect, to pray, and to reminisce always mean to converse with a distant other, without whom the psychic vault would ring hollow.

The home is thus a place that has become fundamental for reflection: the opposition between heaven and earth, high and low, has been replaced by that of one's own home and the homes of others. No action on the world is possible unless it originates from this fundamental little homeland that is a bedroom, an apartment, a house. But there's a difference between fleeing the world and momentarily setting it aside. Shutting yourself away in a room does not mean abandoning the outside world: it means putting it on hold so as to return to it in a better way. If the house becomes an isolation cell, it destroys the enthralling physical engagement we have with reality; it ceases to be a dwelling and becomes a bunker, a fortified encampment.

CHAPTER 7

The Beauty of One's Own Home

Intimacy is also a recent invention, appearing at the end of the eighteenth century in the milieu of the rising bourgeoisie, hand in hand with the emergence of amorous feelings in marriage. For a long time in France and all of Europe, among the rich and poor alike, for both peasants and artisans, the home was communal. We didn't belong to ourselves, and the notion of an individual living apart from the gaze of others made no sense (this is still the case today in a traditional society such as India, where each person remains the property of his caste, his family, his village). Parents and children slept together in the most miserable homes, sometimes in shared beds, with no separation for spouses. The aristocracy, and especially the king, at least in France, were hardly better off by today's standards; all of their functions, including the most organic ones, took place in the presence of witnesses: this was the famous "burden of the commode," a Renaissance invention, which for many was a sign of distinction and disdain toward guests (in a famous passage, Saint-Simon recounts that the Duc de Vendôme, a great soldier, had hardly risen from his bed before settling down on this "unroyal throne" and, in full view of everyone, received relatives and courtiers without embarrassment, imposing his organic functions on them and handing off the basin, once it was full, under everyone's nose). According to historian Michelle Perrot, Louis XIV's bedroom was a cosmic space, meant to embody the universe, the beating heart of the monarchy and therefore of the nation. But it was also a theatrical stage: both when he got up and when he went to bed, crowds of courtiers flocked to his bedside to see him and speak to him according to rites governed by a strict etiquette.[1] Visitors bowed to the royal bed even when it was empty, just as one crosses oneself before the altar in a church. (As for our own times, Clément Rosset recounts that Lacan's worshippers would come to his seminar room on the rue d'Ulm even when he wasn't there, to venerate the Master in his absence.) A retinue of servants, usually male, looked after his nightgowns, wardrobe, chausses, and footwear, supervised by a "first gentleman." The word "bedroom" did not appear until the eighteenth century. The monarch is the property of those around him, except when he joins his mistresses or his official wife, for within him are combined the physical body and the mystical body, the permanence of lineage and its temporary incarnation. "The king lacks nothing but the pleasures of a private life," as La Bruyère astutely wrote.

This private life has been developing at least since the Renaissance, since it accompanies the very process of civilization, as Norbert Elias has conceived it, which first manifests itself in modesty – not spitting, defecating, or making love in front of others – and the withdrawal into the shadows of what was once done in public. The entire nation eventually felt a need for discretion as collective constraints began to seem oppressive in a society won over by the cult of the individual. Modern freedom aspires to free itself from the shackles of the herd, of social status, and of predestination by birth. Little by little, as part of an escape from the oppressive atmosphere of common habitations (still found today in boarding schools, barracks, and mountain huts), enclosed beds were created for spouses, protected by a curtain; in the second half of the twentieth century, Pêr-Jakez Helias referred to them with the term "safe-box for sleeping."[2] A kind of home of one's own was taking shape, as opposed to communal bedrooms, the lot of the destitute and the source of all kinds of abuse, rape, and incest. The poorest slept on the floor, sometimes on vermin-infested bundles of straw, rarely on mattresses; only the privileged had a high bed, sometimes accessible by a stepladder, and for the more fortunate enhanced by a canopy. The bedroom, especially the marital bedroom, the sphere of rest and voluptuous pleasures, gradually came to be shrouded in sacredness, and those who were not family members entered only on tiptoe, never without permission.

The notion of comfort was first born in England around the turn of the eighteenth century. The castles of lords were often cold and pompous, while the hovels of commoners were unhealthy. For the utilitarian Jeremy Bentham (1748–1832), philosopher of pains and pleasures, as for John Locke (1632–1704), liberal thinker and defender of private property, well-being must prevail over the harshness and pomp of the aristocracy. Emphasis was placed on making everyday life more comfortable: airy rooms, better seats and beds, clean toilets, and efficient heating. Material and technological progress, along with refinements in architecture and decoration, transformed the earthly realm from a vale of tears into a vale of roses. The softening of living conditions reflects the desire to make happiness man's new home, his natural environment, the wonderful earthly homeland that will supplant the eventual heavenly one. Pleasure is no longer a mortal sin to be repelled with horror, but a gift to be graciously received as proof of our humanity. The pleasant and the enjoyable can coexist with piety. Rehabilitating the body means offering it a proper dwelling: it is no longer the fleeting envelope of the soul from which we must detach ourselves, but a friend, our sole earthly vessel that we must tend to, and care for with a multitude of hygienic and medical rules. We have invented upholstery, with all its padding, stuffing, and cushioning, for this body, molding to its form so as to accommodate it. Anything that makes sitting and lying down soft and pleasant must be favored. The insides of our homes are designed such that our lives there are better than they are on the outside.

Before it became an enclosed space that confines us, the bedroom was a conquest that protects and shelters. A refugee, for example, does not live in his own place; he is lodged by others, dependent on public charity and therefore also on the moods of his hosts. To have a place of one's own, even a small room, even a closet in certain large cities, remains a tall order. The price of a square metre in London, New York, or Paris, where dwellings are shrinking at an astonishing rate, is a highly political issue. From the nineteenth century onward, the democratization of housing became essential to save the working class from alcoholism and to provide it with hygiene and sanitation. In the family sphere, the scolded child who is sent to bed, deprived of the company of "grown-ups," later (as an adolescent), demands respect for his privacy, which he defends like a fortress. It is forbidden to enter his turret unless you knock: it's part of his body, and entering without prior consent is tantamount to a transgression, almost a violation. The bedroom is a refuge within which to blossom, to reflect, to regain control of one's life, to make plans, to hide one's loves. But this place that is so prized by artists and writers – Marcel Proust wrote while lying in his bed, and spent his nights surrounded by padded walls, so as not to be disturbed by noise as he filled his pages – is also one of confinement. Its closed doors are the delight of frolicking lovers, of spouses who laze about in the conjugal bed, the same bed where we procreate and where, perhaps, we will die. It is also the space of sick people who must keep to their room, and of the elderly or infirm confined to their homes, not to mention prisoners serving their sentences under house arrest. The conquest of the bedroom was long a feminist theme. *A Room of One's Own* is the title of a famous manifesto by Virginia Woolf: "A woman must have money and a room of her own if she is to write fiction."[3] In this biting, ironic pamphlet, the author reminds us that to escape economic dependency on men, women must be financially emancipated (this was already Jane Austen's obsession).

Montaigne was the first to demand an autonomous space in which to reflect and work. "We should set aside a room, just for ourselves, at the back of the shop, keeping it entirely free and establishing there our true liberty, our principal solitude and asylum."[4] Since time immemorial, men have been the conquerors of the outside world, while women have remained prisoners of domestic tasks and child-rearing, as they still are in almost every society. The stroke of genius of Virginia Woolf, whose title resonates like a slogan, is to have transformed this place of imprisonment into one of emancipation: a room of one's own next to the marital bedroom is a first step toward freedom, a way of no longer being dependent on one's husband, a room apart where neither husband nor children are allowed to enter without special permission. It is the place where a novelist or an artist must shut herself away if she is then to radiate out toward the world. The ivory tower is indispensable for any person who wishes to isolate herself and create. She must choose solitude, rather than having the company of others imposed on her. The profession of writer, but also that of artist or craftsperson, is first and foremost a voluntary internment in which she devotes herself to work and meditation, even if she sometimes receives the reward of public exposure.

CHAPTER 8

The Torments and Delights
of a Life in Shackles

There is thus great joy in having one's own home: when social barriers are everywhere and distance is the rule, the home becomes the place where the tenderness of joined hands and effusions of warmth are conserved. And yet, as we see in Baudelaire's work, the bedroom is twofold: on the one hand, it is an oriental palace with muslin curtains where "the soul takes a bath of indolence"[1] in a dream of voluptuousness; on the other, it is a filthy garret whose bailiff demands rent on pain of eviction, and which reeks of "the rancid smell of desolation."[2] The bedroom has two potential destinies: either it is a preface to independent living, or it shrinks into a suffocating niche. For a young adult, whether boy or girl, the move from the family apartment to a studio or shared flat is the sign of a freedom being confirmed. You want your own space, different from that of your family, where you'll be master of your own home. Having a key, a bed, a wardrobe, a table, and a washbasin is a luxury at 20, even if you have to share the common rooms with others. It's a space of minimal freedom: the freedom to be silent at home, to see the projection of your mind on the walls, to have a library, a computer, posters, a fridge at your disposal, a closet full of clothes, to come and go as you please. There's always a gravitational force in a dwelling: you settle in and put all your possessions in their place so as to master the present and prepare for the future. But there's a fine line between well-being and sequestration: after all, the bedrooms of the past were sometimes places of captivity where husbands, brothers, and doctors locked up resistant wives and sisters. Intimacy is a marvellous conquest that can turn against its beneficiaries.

There are all kinds of homes: the shell, the cabin (symbol of sylvan nostalgia), the hut, the tent, the igloo, the fortress, the basement, and even the village or "zone to defend."[3] And let's not forget bomb shelters, cellars, sewers, and subway systems in the context of the Second World War or the Cold War, whose function as shelter is again topical with the Russian aggression in Ukraine, and among American and European survivalists. Every habitat is first and foremost a geometrical space, a dialogue with the outside world. It was Rousseau, on Lake Bienne in Switzerland, who discovered the island of Saint-Pierre, a jewel within a jewel box, and enjoyed the "happiness of a man who likes to cut himself off."[4] There, he escaped the society of men and of the mean-spirited, and dreamed of being confined there for life, so that he might "make this refuge a perpetual prison."[5] Lying on a boat and letting himself drift, he takes joy in himself and his own existence, in a perfect state of happiness that "leaves in the soul no emptiness that it might feel a need to fulfill."[6] It was Flaubert, evoking the vocation and almost the priestliness of the writer, who wrote in his correspondence: "You have to close your doors and windows, curl up like a hedgehog, light a roaring fire in your fireplace because it's cold, and pluck some great idea from your heart."[7]

And here is Bachelard imagining an ideal home by the water: "I also had to have a narrow window, because the smaller the window the better and farther this eye of the house can see."[8] Today, curling up at home also means extending oneself like a radar receiving broadcasts from all over the world, with both hands tapping on the keyboard, the remote control, and the smartphone. We live our lives online – what a strange expression. In the old days, writing lines was a form of punishment at school. Now when we speak of lines, it means being connected to the world via codes. From within this intimate agora, we speak to everyone while remaining alone and immobile. You both act and spectate upon the outside world from the comfort of your own home. Aristotle distinguished the *vita activa* from the *vita contemplativa*. We would need to invent a third category for our own time: the *vita virtualis*, the transformation of the apartment or the house into a microcosm that absorbs the macrocosm and renders it superfluous – a hiding place that holds all the treasures within itself. In the warmth of the cave, protected from the elements, we regard what comes from afar not as the light of Ideas but as the darkness of contingency.

To move into an apartment is first and foremost to put one's own stamp on it, to release it from the spell of anonymity, to exorcise its prior presences. As we've known since the Gothic novel, all rooms are haunted, and we need to break their hexes in order to make them our own. Even hotel rooms, though they are interchangeable and identical, are no exception to our desire for appropriation. Every inhabited space is an atmosphere that repels or attracts. The challenge is thus to unwrap them, as Gide said of Montaigne. But the conquest of the bedroom can turn into a curse. It's a bit like the fate of the famous feminist slogan of the 1960s: my body belongs to me. This is entirely correct. But if my body belongs only to me – if no one else wants it, wants to explore it, share it, celebrate it – this exclusive property ends up weighing me down. Annie Ernaux, speaking of how she was a victim of pickpocketing in a Paris department store at the age of 43, and of how she was vaguely seduced by the young burglar's rough look, says: "The real humiliation, however, was that so much confidence, expertise and longing was channelled toward my handbag and not my body."[9] A place of my own: but if I'm alone in my own home, with no visitors, friends, or children, the walls reflect nothing but my abandonment. The sanctuary becomes a prison. I bump into myself every time I turn a corner. It was the curse of the pandemic to reduce us to the Inside, especially for the elderly and those in quarantine. If there is no more Outside, the Inside loses its *raison d'être*: it becomes an enclosed place without anything beyond it. The great light of the world, the beauty of surprise, no longer irrigate it in an incessant coming and going. The spatial lockdown was first and foremost a mental lockdown.

For a number of years now, American campuses, home of all modern pathologies, have been inventing what we might call "bubbleism." Women or members of minority groups feel the need to keep to themselves in "safe spaces" that are off-limits to intruders. A pox on expansion and self-growth: we must devote our efforts to protecting ourselves from all aggression. The slightest allusion to the traumas of the past – slavery, exploitation, sexism – brings despair to young and fragile minds. Human beings shouldn't be exposed to the open air, but protected from its drafts. In the same way, communitarianism, on which all electoral calculations are based, is a way of withdrawing into one's own clan, faith, or ethnic group to avoid being ruffled by other mores and ways of doing things. Similarly, the move toward "peaceful cities" advocated by certain mayors in Europe runs the risk of transforming our urban communities into necropolises or aseptic spaces: for a big city to be appealing, it must be lively and bustling. The bedroom, like the house, can only serve as a lung if it opens onto the outside world: only in this way can it expand and allow for circulation. As soon as doors and windows remain closed, the lung atrophies and breathes stale air. Whence the pathology of the "bush people" (*lioudi kouski*) in Ukraine, rooted in their homes and reluctant to move, even in a time of war. We must always orient ourselves toward "a metaphysics of the half-open," as Gaston Bachelard put it, to give ourselves the possibility of a future – of fertile accidents. *Living always means living on the threshold*, in an opening that ensures comings and goings. The apartment or house is only an extension of oneself if it overflows into the surrounding neighbourhood, street, or countryside. It then becomes a brink, and indeed an ear that opens onto what surpasses it, onto new destinies. The utopia of a "world-room" (Emanuele Coccia) is perhaps nothing more than a subterfuge: no house, however rich, can replace the planet, for the simple reason that we don't cross paths with others when we're at home.[10] On the other hand, we know that, as Jules Supervielle said of the Argentine pampas, "too much space suffocates us, much more than if there weren't enough space." The prison can also be outside, in the immensity of the steppe or the ocean, which display an "unchanging horizon." An unlimited space is just as oppressive as a dungeon. In Russia, it is infinite space that guards prisoners: the Gulag was as much about the enormity of distances as the severity of the jailers.

As for the much discussed return to the countryside, this has been a literary commonplace since the eighteenth century, ever since Rousseau discussed the potential of Nature to correct the damage done by culture. Recall what Flaubert's Bouvard shouted after receiving a small inheritance: "We'll retire to the country!";[11] he and Pécuchet then consider all the places where they might go, finally choosing Normandy, where they settle down as gentlemen farmers, as conscientious as they are incompetent. Totalitarian regimes, such as those of Mao Zedong and the Khmer Rouge, turned farming into a horrific punishment for the re-education of those resistant to the beauty of communism. Nature, meant to morally regenerate the new man, ends up killing the most fragile of them. In our democracies, the reunion with this green paradise is itself ambiguous: people move far away from the metropolis, but it's less a radical change than a slight shift, a gentle alternative that doesn't seek to overturn the established order. A confinement that takes place outside. We extract ourselves from noisy cities to lead a quiet existence: random gardening, a patch of green that might come to serve as a shelter in hard times. The garden is an aerated cocoon that encloses as much as anything else, and that can also be wearying. As early as 1887, J. K. Huysmans exploded the myth of country holidays in his novel *Stranded*. A Parisian couple, sick of the capital, seek refuge in a château in Brie with their peasant cousins. But the countryside is sinister: when it's not raining, they're devoured by chiggers, and the peasant cousins turn out to be deceitful rogues. One also finds indoor vegetable gardens in city blocks, illuminated by lights as bright as the sun: radish and bean plants in the living room, orchards on the terrace – a whole range of pocket-sized agriculture. The home is an empire that annexes the outside world and swallows it whole. A little like those towers in works of science fiction that have floors devoted to every landscape in the world (savannahs, deserts, jungles, forests), displaying vertically what ordinary space offers horizontally.

CHAPTER 9

The Land of Sleep: Hypnos and Thanatos

A cradle and a tomb, a delightful nest in which to forget oneself and lose oneself, the site of all forms of audacity and renunciation, the bed marks the indispensable suspension of daytime activities and decency. Sleep, like death, equalizes conditions: king and peasant sleep in the same way – but for one, sleep is a sovereign rest, while for the other, it is the forgetting of a life that is too difficult. "To sleep, and then sleep some more: that is my only wish today. An infamous and disgusting but sincere vow" (Baudelaire). Sleep is a regular fall into the abyss, a little death that regenerates us instead of devouring us like the real death. We curl up in our bed as though it were a second skin, seeking blissful obliteration. "It is in bed that we forget, for half our lives, the sorrows experienced in the other half," said Xavier de Maistre at the end of the eighteenth century. In those days, guests were still welcomed in the family bed. In 1976, the photographer Sophie Calle invited friends and strangers to sleep in her bed and have their photographs taken. The bed once again became a potential living space where one could share a unique experience with companions. This intimate accessory can serve as a social space for entertaining, for eating dinner or breakfast, and can be used in a multitude of ways, as a table, a seat, a praetorium. We recall John Lennon and Yoko Ono receiving journalists from all over the world in their bed at the Amsterdam Hilton on March 25, 1969, to protest against the war in Vietnam and deliver a message of peace. For them, the bed was a symbol of harmony, a pedestal, a platform. Sleeping with someone is more intimate than making love: it's the prelude to total abandonment, to complete immersion.

As a place of rest, the bed always oscillates between insomnia and hypersomnia. With time and age, insomnia becomes a way of life that we have to live with. In its extreme forms, its experience – the impossibility of resting – becomes total, superimposing two states, panic and resurrection. Sleep eludes us when we seek it and overwhelms us when we have to stay awake, leading us to a state of exhaustion. In the wee hours of the morning, night rises up like a verdict without appeal. The slightest worry takes on outlandish proportions, and we feel powerless, crushed by this somber swarm of fears. A recumbent humanity is a disarmed humanity: night gives us over to the powers of angst and dread. The reclining position is that of the destitute. And since we sleep wearing nothing, or next to nothing, we're even more vulnerable if we're surprised: we feel as though we're nailed to a bed of misfortune. But there is also insomnia of enthusiasm, when you're carrying within you so much energy and strength that you no longer have the right to sleep. You have to get up so as to recover not only your spirits but your power. Insomnia is the inability to forget yourself, to relax when you're tired and worn out. We go to bed exhausted, we wearily anticipate how hard it will be the next day, but no matter how much we turn over or change sides, we can't sink into sleep. We rehash a phrase or an idea for hours on end. It's an absurd vigilance that impatiently awaits the moment it will be called off, and by this very fact remains on duty. You become your own predicament.

The nightmare only ends when daylight filters through from behind the shutters: the chime from a public building, the horn of a truck, the snorting of your block like an animal beginning to stir, your house coming back to life with the scampering of rodents, birds chirping or flapping their wings. Light returns like an ally, pale in winter, triumphant in summer, tearing the lazy from the warmth of their sheets. It's a euphoric moment for those who feel like they've come to the edge of the abyss and escaped, intact and still alive. When we open our eyes, we think of Seneca's maxim that we should thank the gods on waking for having allowed us to remain in this world. Waking up is a serenity that has conquered terror. All you have to do is sit up to feel your strength return. We were laid to rest; now we're alive again. Our wrath is appeased and our grudges wiped away. Activity chases away our fatigue. Insomnia isn't always negative: we polish sentences during these fruitless hours, we prepare scathing retorts to those who have humiliated us, we make burning declarations to someone who has captivated us, we find solutions to problems. And sometimes a miracle happens: in the stillness of the night, an idea emerges, a conclusion germinates as a result of cerebral turbulence, a single word illuminates an entire line of reasoning. But this grace is rare – ashes and dust produced by a wavering reason. The creative sparks of the insomniac are sometimes as hollow as the pseudo-intelligence conferred on us by drugs or digital hyper-worlds; the broadening of consciousness turns out to be a blister that bursts like a soap bubble in sunlight. Ever since antiquity, we've known that sleep, far from a minor art, testifies to a life of quality, and that deciphering dreams is a form of chiromancy as old as humanity itself. The most unusual thing that can happen to an insomniac is to realize that, in the end, he has slept well and needs no more. But there is also something miraculous about re-enacting from time to time those long nights of childhood when you slept like a log until past noon. The invention of the comforter in Northern Europe in the Middle Ages and the spring mattress in England around 1826, not to mention the tatami and futon from Asia, are among the invisible revolutions that changed the course of humanity. Ukrainians practice the art of sleeping on beehives: the humming of the bees, according to Andrei Kurkov,[1] fosters a long and serene slumber.

Being content with the hours we actually sleep should be the primary lesson of the domestic arts. There's restorative sleep, the quality of which diminishes with age, and there's also a sleep that's like a refuge or an abyss, which doesn't restore you at all. As for choppy sleep, medical historians tell us that, far from being a symptom of modern depravity, it was the norm under the *Ancien Régime*.[2] At one time, certain cities, such as London, were in full swing at three in the morning. Some people sleep their lives away and experience their sleep as if it were their real existence, turning their bed into a precursor to the shroud. This is the theme of Georges Perec's 1967 novel *A Man Asleep*, a rhapsodic tale of a student whose only remaining link to life is sleep – a total immersion with no future and no past – which is punctuated by nocturnal strolls through Paris: "To want nothing. Just to wait, until there is nothing left to wait for. Just to wander, and to sleep."[3] His notion of time dissolves like the separation between day and night as friends start to desert him. To sleep for sleep's sake is to experience the ultimate emptiness. Waking up is about reattaching ourselves to the world, reweaving the thousand threads that bind us to it. The important thing is to get up on the right foot, to start the day with joy and enthusiasm.

It's important to have sleep discipline, and it would be a great idea to rehabilitate the siesta, which interrupts excessive activity and recharges the brain.

Where do sleepers go while they sleep – while they run, climb, fornicate, and kill? How do we know there aren't bestial images and shocking desires behind their closed eyes? Should we believe or ignore the predictions of dreams? Totalitarian powers have always wanted to govern the dreams of their citizens: this is the subject of Ismail Kadare's marvellous book *The Palace of Dreams*,[4] which tells the story of a secret administration that is in charge of collecting and sorting all the dreams in a certain kingdom, in order to collect and sort the "key dreams" that will allow it to decipher the future and prevent coups d'état, wars, and betrayals. Are nightmares bad omens or, on the contrary, a protection against evil? How can we pick out the meaningful clues in this "ocean of horror"? This desire to decipher and control dreams will undoubtedly be the next objective for the tech giants, who will set up dream clouds so as to keep track of us. When you live with the person you love, falling asleep is a kind of evasion that allows you to escape your loved one's surveillance. The jealous lover observes the sleep of his betrothed and senses her fleeing from him: Proust's Albertine (in *The Captive*) is several people at once, and behind her calm, resting face, she may be deceiving the narrator with another woman. In reality, the captive is a fugitive who rejects her jailer's ambition to subdue her: "I felt that I was touching no more than the sealed envelope of a person who inwardly reached to infinity."[5] He showers her with gifts and buys her expensive clothes, the better to lock her up in a prison of rare materials and fabrics. But his jealousy persists, and gnaws away at him. The sleeper seems to be at the mercy of the one who contemplates her, but this is a false docility that foreshadows her imminent escape: "In keeping her in front of my eyes, in my hands, I had an impression of possessing her entirely which I never had when she was awake."[6] On this sleepy face, he thinks he sees forbidden pleasures and frightening hopes. And rightly so, for one morning Albertine flees, never to return. We're both close to and far from Yasunari Kawabata's *House of the Sleeping Beauties*: virgin teenagers, under the effect of narcotics, offer their nude bodies to the voluptuous contemplation of nostalgic old men who pay to be rejuvenated by this disturbing spectacle. As a child, Oblomov viewed his whole household as being stricken by sleeping sickness: the servants asleep while doing their duties, the dogs dozing in their kennels, and the entire estate deafened by the symphony of snoring.

CHAPTER 10

Digital Wonderland or the Triumph of Slouching?

Albert Hirschman once described the oscillation between the public and the private as an alternation of infatuation and disappointment: the individual citizen, weary of the emptiness of consumerism, takes political action; soon, tired of militant struggle, he retreats into the private sphere, but then re-engages a little later, in a pendular movement.[1] The term "cocooning" was coined in 1987 by the consultant Faith Popcorn (a pseudonym), who was dubbed "the Nostradamus of marketing" and mocked by the media. But the real founder of this concept was the British writer Edward Foster, who, in his short story "The Machine" (1909), imagines a humanity made up of isolated monads, each in its own cell, communicating with others only via electronic devices. Today, it's impossible to say whether we're heading toward a society of solitary existences or toward a collective awakening – a Europe remobilized after the nightmare of Covid and that of the war in Ukraine. Two things have changed since the beginning of the twenty-first century: *a politics of fear, for fear and by way of fear* has emerged on a global scale, driven in particular by the UN and NGOs around climate, terrorism, and pandemics, which is creating a feeling of global insecurity. And even more importantly, a universal connection has been established, a veritable Copernican revolution with a truly vertiginous immensity, which seeks to expand the psyche to the size of the planet. But this enlargement is ambiguous: the internet lessens the importance of others, who come to be present only as effigies, not in flesh and blood. The challenge that dating sites present, for example, is that of moving from the flattering photos of someone who interests you to the real person, who is necessarily imperfect and flawed. The Web claims to resolve the contradiction between abstract man and embodied citizen, between humanity and the humanities. The messianic certainty of saving the world, of bringing universal heritage within everyone's reach, of developing tolerance and solidarity, has been shattered by the awareness of a new form of isolation: as in real life, network users are grouped into clans, tribes, and specific affinities. To all appearances, I elevate my little self to the dimensions of the globe. In reality, I'm stuck with myself: inside of this system, there's no one else except those who resemble me. Our center of gravity is within us, and the world revolves around it. Michel Serres's "Thumbelina"[2] – inspired by millennials tapping out text messages with their thumbs – should instead be called "Slipperina."

Strangely, over the last 20 years we've all become cheap spies, reduced to passwords, access codes, and updates: our daily existence is like a treasure hunt in which paying the electricity bill, drawing money from the bank, or making a doctor's appointment all require a set of tools to unlock the services. Every consumer is an unknowing secret agent, but also a suspect who has to justify himself at all times. And woe betide anyone who fails, for he will be reprimanded and even canceled by algorithms. It's odd to see that so many of the demonstrators who only yesterday were marching against the health pass (referred to as a "Nazi pass" by the most extreme) have accounts on Instagram, Facebook, and TikTok, and can therefore be traced in every corner of their private lives by big tech companies (whether American or Chinese) that are ready to track them down and even ban them if need be. Without realizing it, these people are enthusiastic supporters of the surveillance society. Then there's the virtual dimension, which, as in video games, makes it possible to travel through a beyond that is nowhere, to experience fabulous destinies through your avatars, to become an adventurer, pirate, mercenary, criminal, or gangster, in the total immersion of your helmet. (This opens a legal question: that of whether, in the Metaverse for example, I'll be held responsible for the crimes committed by one of my doubles. Who's to blame? Me or my multiple personalities? Complaints of sexual assault are already surfacing in this simulated reality: in December 2021, a female user claimed her avatar had been sexually assaulted in the online game *Horizon Worlds*.) We invent new identities for ourselves and, as in *Second Life* (a game and social network invented in 2003), gain access to a myriad of imaginary planets by way of global platforms (such as Roblox). It's a parallel life that is sometimes wise and sometimes crazy, very popular with teenagers, where you put on a performance, test your skills, and find new partners.

For brands, it's above all a place of intense speculation. We can buy properties on a virtual plot of land in cryptocurrencies, and try on chic online 3D clothing or test a new car that will then be delivered to us in the real world. A tremendous opportunity, to be sure, but is this a case of self-expansion or a simple duplication of everyday activities? It brings to mind the prescient 1999 film *The Matrix*, the story of a humanity that has been defeated and enslaved by machines – the Matrix of the title – and comes to take what it sees for reality and believe in the freedom of its choices. Even if the franchise later became a hodge-podge of metaphysical reflections and flying ninjas, the first *Matrix* film is the great film of Gnosticism, the tradition of thought for which earthly reality is a deception forged by an evil demiurge. If you want to make people disgusted with this earth, it suffices to parrot what most religions say: that it's a hell or a simulacrum from which we must awaken by any means necessary.

Adventurers once took to the sea. Now they take up their joysticks or put on their virtual reality goggles and lie down. Whether you're wearing sneakers, sandals, or pumps, the joystick lets you put on your seven-league boots and cross parallel universes. Based on this model, we can imagine millions of individuals immersed in sensory chambers, vibrating to the stimuli that are sent to them. Great voyages and heightened sensations would take place in a chair. What do we learn from virtual reality? To remain seated or lying down. *We're taking lessons on sitting.* We need seated – and stale – bodies for a society that has itself gone stale, that aims to keep people quiet at home, the better to rob them of their brains. The screen, whatever else it may be, is truly a *herbal tea for the eyes*: it neither forbids nor commands anything, but renders useless anything that isn't it; it diverts us from everything, including itself. In this respect, the emblem of post-Covid civilization will perhaps be neither rockets, nor skyscrapers, nor nuclear reactors, but rather, more humbly, the "smart" armchair, halfway between chaise longue and bed, with a reclining backrest and connected cables. Will this be the citizen of the twenty-first century – the man slumped in his sensory cage, his auditory and optical prostheses guaranteeing multiple forms of enter-tainment? He will have digital doubles who will experience what he no longer allows himself to experience. And he'll feel terribly alone.

We're all familiar with the extreme case of those pale and remote Japanese teenagers called *hikikikomoris*, who are cut off from the world, glued to their screens day and night, fed on trays slipped under their doors. Their addiction never reaches its saturation point, for they are immersed in what has been called "interactive solitude." For them, the true reality is their computer; the physical world is nothing but a superfluous appendage. In augmented reality headsets, reality disappears as the screen moves closer to the eyes. The trade-off for this forced sitting is excess weight, the universal disease of overfed children and the great pathology of sedentary lifestyles. As we know, food advertisements interspersed between two cartoons are a factor in hypertension and weight gain. This has been called "infobesity": the ingestion of news, images, and food by beings who have become robots. The world of continuous entertainment is the world of saturation: we're incessantly gorged on programs and games. During the pandemic, the French, champions of grazing and marauders of fridges, put on weight, just like people in many other countries. Eat, sleep, and digest: bodies have been reduced to so many organic functions, to muscular and physiological catalepsy. Television series shot over the past few years show actors and actresses inflating as the seasons progress, revealing the effects of the lockdown. The latter seems to have rewritten the script of the 2008 animated film *WALL-E*, a gritty dystopia of an obese humanity exiled to a distant planet, having lost the ability to walk on two feet. In the comfort of a life freed from the shackles of work and administrative control, we keep the world close at hand – thanks to the mouse and the remote control.

The Americans coined the term "couch potato" at the end of the twentieth century to indicate a new kind of mutant, slumped on his sofa and devouring potato chips, a fat baby who stuffs himself through his eyes and mouth and allows himself to be bottle-fed. Television and video games have long been electronic baby-sitters, keeping children and parents glued to their screens, frozen in a compulsive telephagy. What is appealing about these media is that they allow for a distracted form of listening – we can leave them on while we do something else – but they also place us under house arrest, and our consumption of them increases with age, in other words with our progressive loss of autonomy. They are sedatives for nursing-home residents: accommodating ladies-in-waiting who can be summoned and dismissed at will, and who saturate everyday life with noise, sound, and color. And let's not forget the new "smart" machines equipped with both synthesized voices and empathy: talking robots, vacuum cleaners, blenders, coffee makers, and high-end appliances that simulate intimacy in the home all the while that they spy on us.

When we enter the digital universe, we believe we're opening ourselves up to an immense realm, but we end up stupefied by its emptiness, our heads stuffed with images and a torrent of futile intrigues: this "soul of the world" is a balloon that reveals only its own vacuousness. We can also allow ourselves to be pampered by way of our online personifications, who enjoy complete security in a kind of virtual day-care center. The expansion of the human psyche is reduced to a slow haemorrhaging of the self through what we see. Augmented reality, you say? But this augmentation looks an awful lot like an amputation. Traditionally, fiction was a refuge from disillusionment. It compensated for certain disappointments, but also enhanced the appeal of reality, its beauty and its paradoxes. The novel, like cinema and theatre, allows us to live more lives than we could ever experience first-hand. With the virtual, we don't even live a single life, just a 3D artefact of one. It gives us a mere illusion of action, of effort, of struggle, making us believe we're fighting in a war or visiting a foreign country; reading, on the other hand, limits itself to setting our imagination in motion. We experience real physical sensations in a video game, whereas reading, contemplating a painting, or listening to music activates other areas of the brain. In one case, you take part in the plot via the devices of extended reality, while in the other, you remain physically outside. It is also possible to wed the classic format of the novel with visual immersion, reviving the "Choose Your Own Adventure" genre by adding music, images, and movement. In and of itself, the Web forms the entire possible Outside; the material universe becomes nothing more than a residue, a point of departure. You're there without being there, everywhere without being anywhere. This leads to an overwhelming dependency, making the return to reality difficult.

Even an activity as simple as going to the movies has become difficult: why should I leave my house, shut myself up in a darkened theatre with strangers, and watch a potentially mediocre film, when I have an unlimited choice of shows on my own screen (in France, theatre and cinema attendance dropped by almost 40 percent in 2022)? Heaven has the very dimensions of my room. Spending time with people we don't know is no longer a pleasure, but a chore. The great collective rituals – outings, galas, etc. – are likely to fade away, or come to be thought of as otherworldly experiences. Anything that can be done from the comfort of your own couch will take priority over yesterday's activities – seeing films and plays and attending concerts. Especially when today, thanks to apps, you can have meals and even sexual partners delivered to you at will. Singers can already give virtual concerts on gaming platforms, while spectators watch the performance through their avatars. You can also hang paintings by Delacroix, Manet or Van Gogh on the walls of your virtual home, or travel from one place to another in your chair, with polar or desert landscapes scrolling before your eyes. You can even travel through time, visiting a Viking village or a futuristic space station (by "futuristic," I mean everything that will go out of fashion the day after tomorrow). Not only do our networks literally fasten us to our armchairs, they also allow us to possess the infinite universe within our private space. The commercial opportunities are undoubtedly considerable, but isn't this in fact a second-rate miracle? Having a parallel digital identity with avatars and crypto-currency wallets won't make my daily life any more exhilarating. The globe is now nothing more than an immense apartment, like in doll's houses or children's games. It's a sanctuary, a haven of peace where we can extract ourselves from a harmful reality.

If, as Gaston Bachlard said, there is always a tension between the home we live in and the home we dream of – whether we're speaking of a cottage, an apartment, or a palace – then none of these can guarantee us security and adventure at the same time. Once we walk out the door, we confront the outside – the unknown, which can be thrilling but also dangerous. Hannah Arendt speaks of "the 'sad opaqueness' of a private life centred about nothing but itself."[3] To this sadness, the internet has added a pocket-sized visual theatre that is as vast as it is superficial. We think we're expanding ourselves, but we're merely fooling ourselves. Our backside in an armchair, a drink in hand, we debase ourselves by watching violent or atrocious series; we tremble, we shudder, and then we go to bed, calm and reassured. Thus do we suffer the double punishment of passivity and ankylosis.

Kant said that the role of schooling is to teach children to sit still. This is a lesson that we've retained well beyond school age, at a time when the institution has lost its luster. At the end of the previous century, two French cartoonists, Cabu (with his book series *Le Grand Duduche*) and Claire Bretécher (with her comic strip series *Les Frustrés*) took note of a physiological change in humanity: the young were beginning to have hunched shapes. The eco-friendly, pacifist, anti-militarist teenager wallowing in his armchair on the one hand, and the bohemian, bourgeois, post-May-'68, depressed-lefty adults slumped on their sofas on the other, embodied this new anthropological type of *Homo erectus* who can no longer stand up straight. A kind of mental scoliosis had overcome the rich nations. Today, we can see that this anthropological stunting has a powerful ally in digital technology. As early as 1998, a young woman in Washington, DC set up an internet site where you could watch her move about her home 24 hours a day, accompanying her in her most modest tasks – this was the first discreet upheaval in the world of images. But the apogee of voyeurism came in April 2001 with the French reality show *Loft Story* (adapted from the American *Big Brother*), which filmed, day and night, eleven singles who were locked in a loft and surrounded by cameras, except in the toilets. The highlight of the show is a sequence in which Loana and Jean-Édouard make love in an outdoor swimming pool. Since then, the method has become universal, and Instagram, Facebook, and TikTok have endlessly multiplied the number of live recordings of daily life, from showers to meals – not to mention loving embraces, for the most exhibitionist of those filming themselves.

Beyond ostentation, this type of project is driven by a mad dream: *that of filming your life to give it the coherence of a feature film*, and hence to give yourself the illusion of being immersed in a gripping adventure. Ah, the thrill of a boiled egg, the wonder of a quintuple burger waiting on your plate! It's all worthy of a selfie stick, a camera, a zoom lens, and worldwide circulation. Stagings of marital serenity act as certificates of fulfillment. My life is an incredible adventure: breakfast in the morning, a splash in the pool, baby's first tooth, hundreds of likes every time. I'm the master of the world, the captain of my own destiny. In the past, we would hide away at home to avoid being seen, but now we hide so as to show ourselves, to spread through our networks. YouTubers, influencers, and bloggers collect huge sums of money to promote their beauty and fashion tips. I'm the hero of an extraordinary story – myself, by myself and for myself – and I invite you to admire me, like the teenager gyrating on TikTok in his kitchen, instead of dancing with thousands of others in a discotheque. Videos and social networks have taken over the role once held by diaries; but where writing can't help but discriminate, and forces the reader to go through it page by page, the camera records everything: the filling of a garbage can, the emptying of a bathtub, the slow growth of lettuce, the roaring of a vacuum cleaner, not to mention breathless episodes of getting up and going to bed. The fact that we're exposing ourselves to video surveillance is less important than the need for total visibility. At a time when the private sphere is acquiring an outsized importance, we're hauling what up to now had been our most intimate secrets – not to mention the little nothings of everyday life that interest no one but the couple concerned – into the public sphere.

It's the end of secrecy, the pessimists will say. But the secret is already exposed, because it's shared by everyone. And when it's out in the open, you can see conformity as much as originality. Indeed, it's astonishing that we give any status at all to these abysmal routines, that we're taken with inanity as though it were a gripping ordeal. The banality of our lives exudes a strong scent of monasticism, but it's a connected monasticism. Perhaps we should see, in this exhaustive transcription of entire hours and weeks, a desire on the part of young people, and especially young girls, to reassure themselves of the quality of their own lives by affirming that they're all in the same boat. The internet is also the great snitch of our connected lives, revealing, thanks to the boorishness of inconsiderate lovers, nudity and sexual acts born of unfaithfulness; like the Soviet secret services of the good old days, it shames people by displaying their most intimate moments for all to see. What Kafka couldn't have foreseen in his short story "The Burrow" – in which a man buries himself under-ground like a mole, protecting himself from the predators that lie in wait – is that the most intimate acts are now the most exposed acts, thanks to the Web and its networks. It is a theatre that has been offered up to the gaze of the multitudes, all with our consent, and this has a reciprocal effect. The private realm is now completely socialized; of our own free will, our sanctuary is completely exposed. As Pessoa wrote: "I've so externalized myself on the inside that I don't exist there except externally. I'm the empty stage where various actors act out various plays."[4]

"Every exceptional person," writes Nietzsche, "instinc-tively seeks out his fortress, his secrecy, where he is delivered from the crowd, the multitude, the majority, where he is allowed to forget the rule of 'humanity,' being the exception to it."[5] But when this desire for hiding away becomes collective, when it becomes the very mark of the herd, the "exceptional person" must leave the lair, lest he come to resemble the reviled crowd. If the "home of one's own" comes to triumph over public space during the course of this century, there will be as many substitutes for the universe in the intimate space of the home as there are people. The joy of existence will lie in replacing event by atmosphere, the expedition by visual strolls, with the only interruption being that of going from chair to sofa, from bed to bathroom. Our only movement will be from our living room to our kitchen and then back again. Can a freedom without obstacles or the risks of the open air ever be anything more than an ersatz? Will the great theatre of the world disappear, swallowed up by a skylight? Private life once needed the Outside; its only asset was its lack of completion. Now, aided by the infinite lushness of the Web, it has become solipsistic: it is intoxicated by itself and the shadows it takes for reality.

CHAPTER 11

Diderot's Dressing Gown

The triumph of intimacy is first and foremost the return to favor of the domestic arts, and the reappropriation, on the part of men, of activities hitherto associated with women or servants. Above all, it means a commitment to living spaces and the kitchen, and a heightened awareness of everyday objects in all their familiar strangeness. As early as the eighteenth century, certain recalcitrant men trampled on these objects, calling them "knickknacks" (Rousseau), "meager merchandise" (Robespierre), or "trinkets and nonsense" (Adam Smith). A century later, Baudelaire thundered against "the fanatics of the utensil," and Flaubert, in the very midst of the Second Empire, cried out: "We must shout against cheap gloves, against desk armchairs, against the mackintosh, against cheap stoves, against fake cloth, against fake luxury . . . ! Industry has developed ugliness in gigantic proportions!"[1] The joy we now take in cooking at home, maneuvering pots and pans, transforming vegetables, meats, and starches into meals, owning those fabulous new appliances that peel, cook, mix, heat, serve us, and talk to us, in summoning the cosmos into our frying pans, in cleaning our house from top to bottom, in making our beds, doing our laundry, and tidying up is obviously progress, because it's no longer the sole preserve of mothers and wives, but the lot of everyone. The renewed commitment of men to the domestic economy can be experienced by some as a punishment, the end of a privilege, or conversely as an enrichment, an expansion of the self. We enlarge our skill set by focusing on the smallest details. Our new kitchen devices may not have liberated women, but they have made everyday life easier. None of us can escape their minor but healthy prowess, as Boris Vian already noted in his famous 1956 song "Progress Blues," in which he sang of "slug ironers," "spray mixers," and "chicken skinners." We're still fascinated by our robots, our lighting fixtures, our "smart" machines whose instructions require a high IQ from their readers, and we wield brooms, mops, and hammers the way our ancestors wielded swords and halberds. We have to take care of our house, which is a way of taking care of our soul. When order reigns in an apartment, the mind is able to reflect and get itself going.

In this return to the self, the bathrobe, the blanket and the slipper regain their importance. What is a slipper? The domesticated extension of the shoe or boot, the transformation of the walking foot into the sleeping foot: the means of locomotion has become a means of stagnation. It's a cocoon – a round, pleasing niche. The winged foot, when it is wrapped in felt and wool, agrees to rest forever in its cushion of warmth. It is hardly surprising that the market for slippers exploded with the pandemic, causing shortages and supply problems, as was the case with many other goods.[2] Loungers and moccasins have become synonymous with withdrawal and comfort for all. It's hard to imagine heroes, adventurers, and trailblazers wearing them. A life lived with muffled footsteps will always seem less exhilarating than one lived in dress shoes or sneakers, which impose a dynamic rhythm on walkers.[3] Surprising someone you admire – a great artist, a great writer, an unparallelled actor – when he's wearing slippers means catching them in a painful prosaism. It calls to mind Hegel's famous claim: "No man is a hero to his valet; not, however, because the man is not a hero, but because the valet – is a valet."[4] It's true that we live in post-heroic times that are hardly conducive to great deeds: people today aim for the sanctity of the victim rather than the greatness of the intrepid. Anyone who goes out in clogs, flip-flops, or slippers to do their shopping is making a statement: we are indoor beings making a brief incursion to the outside before returning to our homes. As for the bathrobe, it's a light covering that you wear when you get out of bed before putting on something more socially suitable. If you're satisfied with this kind of outfit, doesn't it mean you've abandoned concern for how you look for the sake of simple comfort? Like mercenaries wearing oriental slippers or Amazons in nightgowns, these people shout high and wide that they're content with how they are, even at the expense of letting themselves go. Doesn't being free mean, first and foremost, standing up straight and minding your posture?

The dressing gown has always been an eminently popular item: this indoor coat, which was originally a fashionable men's garment, was used by ladies to cover their sleeping garments, so as to keep out the cold and conceal their bodies. A little literary anecdote: from 1747 to 1765, Diderot wore a blue robe to write certain articles for the *Encyclopedia*. But his benefactress, a certain Madame Geoffrin, well known in Paris's salons, had Diderot's house repainted in his absence, his furniture replaced, and his old robe discarded in favor of one made of luxurious silk. Denis wore it reluctantly, but never stopped mourning the old, worn-out one, to which he would ascribe the highest virtues. This worn-out fabric was like a home to him. "Why didn't I keep her? She was made for me; I was made for her. She hugged the line of every fold of my body without hemming me in. I looked a picture. I looked my best. The other one is stiff and heavy and makes a manikin of me. [. . .] When a book was covered in dust, one of her lapels would come forward to wipe it. When the ink had clogged and refused to flow from my pen, she would offer her skirt. Long black stripes visibly recorded the many favours she had done me. The black stripes were the sign of the critic, the writer, the working man. Now, I look like a rich layabout; nobody knows who I am. [. . .] My old dressing gown was of a piece with the rest of the jumble that used to surround me. [. . .] Now all is discord. The overall effect is lost. There's no longer any unity or beauty."[5] He finds in luxury nothing but ravages: opulence has destroyed the unity of his home; the new robe doesn't go with his old straw chair, his wooden table, his fir plank. Diderot's dressing gown was as much a work tool as a garment for the home: it was the uniform of the craftsman whose job it is to write, who both dirties his hands and stains his outfit. It clothes his body of yesterday, a body that was younger and more dynamic. Diderot thus desacralizes the figure of the artist, painting a picture of a simple, frugal being who isn't precious and doesn't make a fuss when he's at home. The writer is not a sacred being: Diderot's robe, the nightcap of Louis-Sébastien Mercier (1740–1814, a talented and prodigious Enlightenment writer who today is mostly forgotten), Sherlock Holmes's cape, and Oblomov's slippers are the accessories of ordinary men who contradict the pose of the Romantic poet or the cursed artist, dressed in their tail-coats, frocks, jabots, and ascots. These are security blankets for adults, the transitional objects that Winnicott spoke of and that enable us to tame the world. Today, Diderot would write in shorts or a tracksuit. At least his robe fetish didn't prevent him from traveling far and wide, by the standards of his time: he visited Catherine the Great in Moscow and embraced the vast world with an optimism and an ardour that we no longer possess. A more recent example: throughout the Second World War, Winston Churchill led Britain from his bed "with a mixture of eccentricity and panache."[6] His red and gold robe, which made him look like a Chinese mandarin, became an emblem of the Prime Minister's resistance to Nazi barbarism.

I've just quoted from Fagan and Durrani's "horizontal history" of humanity. One day, someone will write a seated history of humanity, of the body that sprawls or hunches over, hugging the curves of a deck chair or an armchair: a new animal, prostrate on its seat, halfway between lying in bed and standing up. Traditionally, going out to work or to walk meant getting ready and being attentive to your dress. As Levinas states: "The most delicate social relations are carried out by way of forms."[7] The risk of carrying your inner self around with you is that of looking a mess, of refusing to go to any lengths for others: you show yourself as you are, you let your guard down, you couldn't care less about being judged. To quote an ad for McDonald's in France: "Come as you are." You're supposed to be who you are, without any fuss. But *leaving home always means leaving yourself*, and thus dressing properly, making yourself look good for others. Kamel Daoud, in a series of exchanges with Raymond Depardon about his country, calls Algeria "a country that has shut itself away, in which only members of the group interact, and where everyone walks around in slippers and pyjamas."[8] Dictatorships depoliticize their citizens and deny them access to the world, conditioning them to not even getting dressed. But when it's the turn of democracies to fall ill, negligence and sloppiness become the norm. The risk? That since the pandemic, the private sphere has come to invade the public sphere: everyone strolls around in slippers, shorts, and T-shirts, indifferent to judgments and resistant to codes. Like those people who go out in their pyjamas on Sundays to buy croissants, a little weekend bending of the work-week rules. We know that tracksuits have long been the uniform of football and rugby fans, sprawled out on the sofa munching peanuts and drinking beer. It's a sort of minor mimicry of the players who toil on the pitch. But while it's nice to be comfortable, you can't build a civilization on softness alone. In the years to come, there will undoubtedly be a strong reaction to this laissez-faire attitude: a surge of formalism, an explosion of dandyism, an appetite for chic attire to ward off the general softening.

CHAPTER 12

Those Who Have Deserted Modernity

Standing before the ills that currently overwhelm us, how can we not evoke a little-known literary trend of the nineteenth century, which resists both Romantic pathos and elite conservatism? In the aftermath of the French Revolution, Europe seemed to be divided into two camps: on the one hand, the merchants and entrepreneurs who worked, hoarded, and obeyed the logic of calculation; on the other, the rebels, themselves divided between bohemians and revolutionaries, who rose up against the new capitalist order, loathing bourgeois mediocrity and its oppressive norms. Anarchists, republicans, and socialists protested politically, while both great and mediocre artists did so aesthetically. But a third camp, smaller than the other two, emerged from this confrontation: those who deserted life. These refuseniks neither revolt nor work. They refute their century and *go on strike against existence*, each in his own way. While Romanticism, at first accused of being a *trompe-l'oeil* of capitalist exploitation, moved to the left as early as 1830, they went nowhere. The deserter refutes both the bourgeois and the anti-bourgeois. They go back and forth between supine life and aborted life.

These ungrateful sons of revolutionary turmoil seek not to sow the future but to sterilize it. They don't have an overarching theory or belong to a single school, but form a tendency that has run through much of their work over the past two centuries, from Xavier de Maistre to Georges Perec, via Dostoyevsky, Sartre, Beckett, and Kafka (though none of them falls completely within this current). Their only passion is to kill passion, their only desire to stifle desire. Even the mediocrity of the universal petty bourgeois strikes them as too convulsive: these commoners aspire to absolute calm. They form an ideal antidote to the madness of the modern world, but without proclamation or manifesto: their only drive is to cool things down. These activists of banality insist on the truth of inaction and the greatness of immobility – what Michel Houellebecq calls "existence at low altitude."[1]

The first French writer to sing the praises of the indoors was Xavier de Maistre, in his 1795 book *Voyage around My Room*. Taking the opposite tack to tales of peregrination or heroic conquest, he wrote this book while being held prisoner in Turin as a result of a duel with a Piedmontese officer. A sort of anti-Rousseau who was a tireless wanderer (he roamed across much of Europe on foot), de Maistre, sentenced by a court to stay in a luxurious room with a servant, describes all the charms of this experience in the text's 42 chapters: his bed and his wardrobe, his dog Rosine and his valet Joanetti, his abundant library and the etchings on his wall. The bedroom becomes the true hero of the book, offering up to the writer an inventory of its treasures, with each object and each piece of furniture serving as the theme of reveries and meditations (Victor Hugo drew inspiration from de Maistre in his *Last Day of a Condemned Man*). This immobile journey is a response to the historical traumas caused by the French Revolution.

As in Boccaccio's *Decameron*, a series of 100 libertine short stories recounting the love affairs of young people who took refuge in the countryside to escape the Black Death that ravaged Florence in 1348, Xavier de Maistre celebrates the happy enclosure that protects against the ugliness of the world. As a prisoner, he understands that even the most unfortunate human being, provided he has a nook in which to take refuge, can slip away through reading, imagination, and dreams without feeling miserable or diminished. The advantages of traveling in place are multiple: it doesn't cost anything, doesn't put the traveler at any risk, and is suitable for the destitute, the cowardly, and the idle. "Let all the lazy arise en masse,"[2] de Maistre writes – to go nowhere. His room-based imagination, which leads from bed to armchair and from armchair to entrance hall, and favours the oblique over the straight line, is both cheerful and impoverished:

> A nice fire, books, pens; how many resources there are against boredom! And what a pleasure it is, too, to forget your books and your pens and instead poke your fire, succumbing to a gentle contemplation, or arranging a few rhymes to amuse your friends! Then the hours slip away over you, and silently fall into eternity, without making you feel their melancholy passage.[3]

In the warmth of his bed, the author meditates and transports himself, by way of the mind, to the most fabulous lands. As we flip through this book, we have the sense that we're reading one of the many "Lockdown Diaries" that peppered the year 2020. The bedroom is the starting point for many potential journeys that will never take place. De Maistre sheds a tear over the devotion of his servant and the faithfulness of his dog, and contemplates the portrait of an elegant duchess who allows his soul to "sweep across a hundred million leagues in a single instant."[4] In his mind, he speaks to illustrious scholars and figures from ancient Greece such as Plato. Notwithstanding the humor that is scattered across the narrative, which seems to become more of a self-parody with each passing page, this *Voyage* cultivates artificial ecstasy and fake amazement. A nostalgia for escape is evident in this eulogy of confinement: the author is making the best of a bad situation.[5] Inspired by Sterne's *Sentimental Journey through France and Italy*, de Maistre founded an entire literary trend of autobiographical introspection. This ironic work has subsequently been parodied a thousand times over: in 1798, there even appeared a text entitled *Voyage in My Pocket*.

We see something similar in the present day: as we confront the convulsions of History, there is a great temptation to take refuge in small spaces where we can control every square meter. Those who are frightened by the world imagine themselves as stylites living atop their pillars or as wealthy hermits. Like Xavier de Maistre, they proclaim the bedroom as "that delightful country that holds every good thing, and all the riches of life, within its realm."[6] The way we think about bedrooms is close to how we think about prisons, even if the conditions associated with these spaces are very different. We know that many ex-prisoners carry prison around with them, reconstituting it even after they've been released, to the point that it permeates their daily lives and sticks to their skin. They may even idealize it, remembering it as a sort of Eden: Jean Genet's great talent was to transform the rogues and criminals he came across in prison into princes, aristocrats, and geniuses of poetry and delicacy. Queers, whores, and beggars became a new nobility in his writing: they speak like François Villon or the Princesse de Clèves. There is also an entire literature of sanatoria, which found its highest exemplar in Thomas Mann's *Magic Mountain*, a novel of thwarted love affairs and battles of ideas undertaken from deckchairs, but also a condemnation of the earthly realm, which is about to tumble into war (the novel is set during the eve of the First World War). In nursing homes, hives of debate and intrigue, sociability depends on the state of lungs or the virulence of a cough, and residents are divided between the magnificent condemned ones, who will be discreetly evacuated, and the survivors, who resist and bear witness.

We shouldn't dismiss the devious pleasure of getting bogged down in everyday life as though it were the sands of a desert. There are many people who have answered the enigmatic question of how not to live in ways that are very original, and that depend on their era and their sensibility. The Swiss writer Henri-Frédéric Amiel (1821–81) fascinatingly embodies our own experience, which is weak in events. In the truly monstrous diary (it is over 17,000 pages long) that this professor of aesthetics and literature at the University of Geneva kept throughout his life, he recorded the trivial things he went through with a singular meticulousness (there are a great many observations about the weather); his days are characterized by the fact that little or nothing happens. The charm of any given day lies in the small, purely nominal difference separating it from the day before and the day after. Things are endlessly repeated, but with tiny distinctions that make each one unique. Aside from the biological regularity of meals, which breaks up the monotony of the hours, the writing of the *Diary* consists in a recording of each successive interval. Amiel was a multifaceted man: a great scholar, a professor of literature, and a highly regarded social figure, he actually led a double life – the official one and the one he dreamt up. In the latter, he imagined the books he might have written, the women he might have married (his emotional life was reduced to a bare minimum), the journeys he might have undertaken. At once fanatical and weak-willed, caught up in what one might call "the universal transformability of the possible," he strove to always remain in the wings of existence; only his meticulously kept *Diary* gave him the illusion of truly living. There were and are other diarists, but he alone stamped insipidity with a steadfastness that should earn him a title: emperor of the atonal.

Even more than de Maistre, who was a great soldier and a great traveler, Amiel took the promotion of insignificance to a new level. Insignificance in this context is not the uninteresting or the futile, but that which has not yet been given meaning. It's an exploration of details, a commitment to making something novelistic out of nothing. His diary is a paper sanctuary dedicated to a new divinity, one that has emerged triumphant in autofiction: the infinitesimal, which he strives to stage and to illuminate. Moods, anecdotes, migraines, painful digestion, breathing difficulties, wonder at the play of light on Lake Geneva, various ailments – all the little things that make up the menial prose of life end up composing an adventure. His obsession is to make timetables, to lock up the future in the calendar's prisons. Filling entire hours is difficult; if you can't do it, you can always divide them into minutes: "It took me almost eight hours in a row," he writes, "to construct a chart for the use of my time this winter." What is at stake is not merely the perverse project of planning one's life in order not to live it, but also an attempt to escape the grasp of the present by dreaming of mastering it in the future. We imprison our weeks in the rigid corset of a schedule to ensure that we have a place in it, that we're expected there, that there won't be any unpleasant surprises. Amiel's great successor today is the Norwegian writer Karl Ove Knausgård and his 4,000-page confession *My Struggle*, which deals in a total realism; its dazzling success is a testament to the prevailing climate of our time: the preference for authenticity over fiction.

It's worth taking another look at Herman Melville's 1853 story "Bartleby, the Scrivener," whose eponymous hero begins as a conscientious paper-pusher who turns into a sad slug. The copyist is the great negative hero of the nineteenth century, heir to the medieval monks, and when he rebels against his fate, like Bouvard and Pécuchet seeking to compile all the knowledge of their time, he ends up wearily returning to his scribbling trade. Bartleby works in a Wall Street office until he declines his boss's requests with his famous remark: "I would prefer not to." This strange affirmative negation has intrigued generations of philosophers and literati: this scribe, whose office faces a brick wall and who ends up in prison, is, in his own way, a Lilliputian colossus. Pallid as a corpse, he is assigned modest tasks at his modest workbench; as such, he is different from Bouvard and Pécuchet, who are possessed by an insane lust for knowledge. Bartleby is a story of aggressive passivity, of a man who wears down his boss and colleagues with his resistance and his gloomy arrogance: right to the denouement, he employs *the eccentricity of the dull*. This paper-pusher, formerly a clerk at the Dead Letter Office in Washington, copies life to avoid living it. As Gilles Deleuze suggests, he chews on writing that has already been written, but this menial activity soon exasperates him, and he stops writing so as to squat on his boss's premises, where he embeds himself until he is evicted. Collating documents, copying them, passing them on: monks once performed this task in the shadows of their monasteries, saving thousands of Greco-Latin texts from oblivion. Bartleby inhabits a space that is somewhere between Plato's cave (but without the least interplay between light and shadow) and a monk's cell, transposed into the dusty decor of a nineteenth-century office: nowadays, he'd be an OpenSpace or FlexOffice programmer in an anonymous building. Bartleby copies "silently, palely, mechanically,"[7] and, at the slightest request from his colleagues or superiors, utters the formula that drives them mad: "I would prefer not to." His silence provokes an abundance of comments and exasperation. Little by little, this man whose soul is on strike, as Jean-Louis Bory put it, gives up all activity, is chased out of the office, and ends up in prison. *Preferring not to means refusing both acceptance and refusal – choosing "no" while mitigating it without canceling it out.* It's the phrase that rejects all others; when he has finished uttering it, Bartleby goes silent once and for all. Melville was not only the author of this immense little book, to use Jacques Derrida's felicitous phrase: he was also the writer of liquid gigantism, in the figure of the white whale in *Moby-Dick*; like all novelists, he discovered new continents in both the infinitely large and the infinitely small, and, with Bartleby, he explored the excess of the minuscule, at once anemic and virulent.

CHAPTER 13

Weather Sorrow

Following in the footsteps of Jean-Jacques Rousseau and Maine de Biran, Henri-Frédéric Amiel invented what was to become the leitmotif of the centuries to come: a passionate interest in the weather as it relates to our moods. Before him, the Ancients and then Montesquieu had already studied the influence of the climate on political regimes. Amiel systematized atmospheric notations, starting each entry in his *Journal* with an indication about the current weather – as if one had to consult the sky to know how to feel: "Overcast. The heat wave seems to have broken." "Grey or cold sky, lacking any rays of sunlight, lacking love, just like the disenchanted life of one who has never dared to reach out his hand to a woman and say: 'Under God's watch, will you make this crossing with me, and bind yourself to me with a solemn oath?'" "Sky flecked with grey and creased with various shades, fog trailing over the mountains of the horizon; melancholy nature, leaves falling on all sides like the last illusions of youth beneath the tears of incurable sorrows [. . .] The fir tree, alone vigorous, green, stoic in the midst of this universal phthisis." And again: "Beautiful sunshine floods my room, nature is celebrating, autumn is smiling. I respond to these overtures as best I can."[1]

The role played by the weather is double: it either thwarts our mood or accompanies it. It is a corrector or an amplifier, dictating our conduct, inviting us to go out, or discouraging us from taking to the road or sea. Weather forecasting was born at the junction of the eighteenth and nineteenth centuries, when it went from being a science of rural and maritime previsions to one of intimacy – of moods. What is a mood, if not a relationship between the world and ourselves that brings wavering and helpless beings face to face with an ever changing nature? In making us accustomed to small variations in temperature and to the hues of the sky, the weather constitutes a pedagogy of diversity: if nothing happens to us, it will at least happen that it rains, that it's windy, that the sun shines. It is the minimal adventure that affects each of us. The charm of the weather lies in its irregularity, its kaleidoscopic variability. As it makes us more sensitive, it accustoms us to living within an ethics of halftone and nuance. Weather is an educator of perception. And since the passage from hot to cold, and from one season to the next, allows us to feel our existence, the weather resurrects the Greek idea of the cosmos: a solidarity between the elements and the human heart, a communion for which our love of feeling like part of a larger whole makes us nostalgic.

But this solidarity has become fissured since the beginning of the century: we've moved from the theory of climates to the theory of climate disruption. In the eighteenth century, the Encyclopedists relied on geographical determinism, stressing the emollient nature of warm countries, which encourage sensuality and laziness, and the rigidity of cold countries, which are conducive to work and moral rigor. This no longer holds. The weather is now the result of what we have caused, by way of our excesses, to come undone: the consubstantial link between man and nature, between microcosm and macrocosm, has cracked. Weather is no longer the barometer of the soul, but the thermometer of human madness; it has become a science of warning and even alarm. No respite, no rest: sunny or rainy, the weather underscores the threat toward which we're inexorably heading. Linking the world outside to our intimate inner worlds, weather forecasting has been, since the 1950s, the hedonic symbol of developed nations: summer led us to the beach, winter to the snow. Behind the smiles of the presenters now lurks a danger. The possible collapse of the polar ice caps, record-breaking temperatures in Alaska and Greenland in July and August, arctic cold and blizzards in Texas – in short, a general disruption that reflects our own confusion. The world has blown a fuse. Amiel is, along with Rousseau, one of the great authors of meteorological sensibility, and we owe him this now-famous phrase: "Every landscape is a state of soul." Our soul is now disjointed.

Hegel once said that reading the newspaper is our morning prayer. But the weather forecast is our prayer all day and all night. In most countries, it is presented by women, often young, whose facial expressions give away whether the news is good or bad. A frown and it's rain and grey skies. A smile is a promise of sunlight and warmth. The ideal weather should combine moderation and contrast. When showers and cold dominate, journalists become the bearers of bad news, and we vilify them. At the turn of the century, in some Eastern European countries, weather presenters took off their clothes on screen as summer approached, to convey a message of lightness and pleasure. Whatever the circumstances, forecasting requires the seriousness of prognostication and the solicitude of the declaration: dress warmly in snowy and icy weather; bring your umbrella if you're in northern Europe, and

your wool sweater if you're heading for Scandinavia. But
the jaunty tone of classic weather forecasting is no longer
permitted. Climate is war, and the carefree are potential
criminals. Every announcement must be accompanied by
seriousness to avoid accusations of irresponsibility. When
it's time for the weather forecast, the death knell sounds.
In the past, disturbances and even disasters were brief or
exceptional. Now, the seasons succeed one another willy-
nilly: snowstorms in Greece, and "winter heatwaves"
in California in February, with temperatures of 30 °C
– meteorologists have dubbed these phenomena "delight-
mares." Today, the very sun that bathes your vacations in
light conceals a potential drought or heatwave. The blue
sky is a deceptive climatic bomb, ready to explode with
fires, storms, and devastating floods. No one is spared,
regardless of where he lives.

Since the weather is the skin of the world, the primordial
garment I discover when I get up in the morning, I run
the risk of feeling permanently uncomfortable in my skin.
Certain nervous systems pick up on the nuances of the
atmosphere with an almost electric sensitivity, and the
slightest cloud or fog brings with it an entire grueling
drama: since 1987, a new term, SAD, Seasonal Affective
Disorder, has been added to the forms of chronic depression
listed in the DSM (*Diagnostic and Statistical Manual of
Mental Disorders*, published by the American Psychiatric
Association). Meteorology took several centuries to break
away from the popular beliefs that chalked floods, volcanic
eruptions, and earthquakes up to the fury of the gods.[2] A
great cosmic body bathes our organisms, drawing us into
its tremors, sighs, and storms, inflicting its pathologies
on us, and allowing us to benefit from its bright spells.
But this great body is now ill. Modern civilization has
crushed an ancestral balance, and nature is taking revenge
for our negligence. If sunlight expands our souls to their

furthest reaches, while grey or leaden skies make our hearts contract, the message of climate disruption is this: stay at home, if possible – don't add to humanity's carbon debt by traveling. In France, we're told to replace our pilgrimages with what have come to be called *mobilités* – a lovely gimmick of a word that asks you not to move beyond a certain perimeter. *The torments of the skies have always been a personal tragedy; now, the climate's spasms are a tragedy for the whole of humanity.* The latter is condemned, time is running out, and young people are suffering from "eco-anxiety." Their misfortune is directly linked to the convulsions of a planet in its death throes. This little spaceship carrying us as it moans proves that we no longer belong on this Earth: we've destroyed our habitat and we've also destroyed ourselves. The obsolescence of the human race has been proclaimed, as the German philosopher Günther Anders already said in the twentieth century: we've passed from the time of revolutions to the time of catastrophes. The blissful ignorance of the post-war period is now forgotten: the good times are over.

In contrast to the cathartic function of ancient rituals, which expelled aggressive impulses, our secular rituals, which dramatize the status quo and force us to live within the terrifying imminence of a cataclysm, have an anxiety-provoking function. Faced with an ever increasing number of violent storms, will we, like many other peoples on this Earth, be able to acquire the intelligence that is grounded in adversity, or will we continue to expect the State to do everything – bottle-feed us, cajole us, advise us, and console us? Climatic calamities have always existed. But in the past, they were linked to divine wrath. Now we know that they derive from the Anthropocene – from human insanity. Global warming has become the Swiss army knife of causality. It has an answer for everything, whether it be storms, riots, famines, or terrorism; it shares with God the peculiar feature of allowing us to invoke it whenever we want to explain anything we want. It unites learned discourse with popular fears and even superstition. Weather forecasting is a science, but it is no less a daily sermon – an admonition and a warning from Gaia, who punishes us for our excesses with vile catastrophes. By way of its predictions, a merciless Nemesis punishes each of us for the faults of humanity as a whole.

The excesses of our industrial societies result in cyclones, epidemics, tidal waves, and typhoons (which are given alternately feminine and masculine names to avoid offending anyone). At the end of March 2020, a former French Minister of Ecology proclaimed that Covid was nature's last warning to a debauched humanity before the final punishment. In its everyday banality, weather conceals fury and revenge. What its forecasts express is a sentence: what we will need to do to achieve expiation. It remains to be seen – the entire theory of the Anthropocene is based on this premise – whether we will be able, by way of divestment and deprivation, to curb our march toward global warming. Even if we achieve carbon neutrality by the middle of the century, it's a safe bet that climate disruption will continue for a long time yet, simply through inertia. We're still not even able to make it snow or rain, so how are we supposed to control the entire globe? A Promethean vision of the world still reigns in political ecology, one that combines repentance with megalomania: it's enough to want something to make it possible. It's a safe bet that our incapacity to turn things around immediately, and our tendency to overestimate our omnipotence, will provoke even more fury and despair among the militants of the Apocalypse. If we're no more masters of the climate than of ourselves, it would seem that the only choice, in the end, is that of a sedentary lifestyle.

CHAPTER 14

Existential Defeatism

Modernity is full of heroes of extinction and dormition, who deploy an exorbitant force of inertia, setting forth lethargy and laziness as absolute values. For them, existence is akin to subtraction. Real life – the storms you desire, the pathos of intensity – is a chimera for them, like the modern slogans dear to managerial advertising: "You must change your life." And while, on the one hand, the quest for reaching great heights has continued unabated throughout modernity, from Romanticism to Situationism (and without forgetting Rimbaud), the *Decelerators* move to the beat of a different drummer, asserting a sort of existential defeatism. By choosing not to live, they strip the ideal of happiness of the thick gilt veneer that once covered it. They reject the model of the prophet and the rebel because they see themselves as priests of the small, of wilful inaction. They are not heroes of the light or of frenetic movement, but exhibitionists of nothingness, enthusiasts of willful lethargy. What they end up constructing in spite of themselves is *a stunted romanticism* in which they meticulously craft a project of being nothing. Perhaps in the future this program of reduction will be adopted by everyone, or at least part of the population, should the seductions of larval life prevail. This singular reversal also governs the writing of autofiction, invented by the literature professor Serge Doubrovsky in the 1970s: rather than recounting what we have lived through, we write to persuade ourselves that we are alive. We do so in order to amplify ourselves, even in the most minimal of ways, and we are astonished by the inexhaustible richness concealed in such a seemingly mediocre life. The intimate – or rather infinitesimal – diary claims to exhaust reality in its entirety. It invents its own readers – brothers and sisters in inconsistency. Gathering your meager pickings week after week so as to create a daily inventory of your own banality is a formidable challenge. You have to consist in yourself minute after minute, confronting the storm of listless hours in which the ego is at risk of dissolving. I am unfathomably deep, Henri-Frédéric Amiel once said, because over the course of the year's 365 days, I live 365 different destinies. The day as the totality of human drama is a major theme of the modern novel, from James Joyce to Virginia Woolf, not to mention Katherine Mansfield, and, in our time, Annie Ernaux or Marguerite Duras. The professor from Geneva may very well be tired of living, but the fatigue in question is hyperactive, as our exhausted man creates a treasure trove of energy to ensure that nothing happens to him. There are no limits to banality: this is what he discovers as he plunges into the vertiginous microcosm of his vacuity. Even in this small territory, I have no sovereignty, for I am overwhelmed. Not living is a Herculean task. The reticence of Lilliputian fanatics is a monumental labor. Shrinking, for them, is a form of passion.

And it's true that passion is necessary to endure this form of daily existence: those who lead reclusive lives offer themselves up far more than others to the terrible god of boredom. The latter possesses an erosive power that blunts and swallows up life's adventures. The metaphors to which it gives rise are those of bogging down, seizing up, coagulating: a ship caught in the ice and forever immobilized for Baudelaire and Poe; a motionless marsh for Flaubert; a barren glacier that paralyzes a bird for Mallarmé; a dreary plain beneath the snow in winter for Verlaine and Chekhov; a limestone deposit that ends up clogging pipes for Moravia; the viscosity of a nature that engulfs you for Sartre (in *Nausea*). To be bored is in some way to remain stuck to oneself, with no possible escape. You go from being to almost being, enduring the insipid flow of a time deprived of meaning. Boredom is the best example of a disease of interstices, for it seeps into the smallest moments like an aspic that comes to freeze existence, lining the alveoli of consciousness and preventing any impetus. It turns existence into a mere interval between experiences of nothingness, and social networks amplify this feeling of emptiness online the world over.

For a long time, the provinces, in France just as in Russia, formed the metaphysical category of boredom par excellence. They represented a low-lying life, an interminable hibernation whose fascinating insipidity the best writers, from Chekhov to Sartre, have ingeniously described for centuries. With global lockdown, and its pitiful bare-bones existence, this bleak life of being crammed within the walls of an apartment became, for a while, the life of all. Wearing slippers or tracksuits, confined within an assigned walking area, we have been asked to renounce everything on earth having to do with astonishment, novelty, and the unknown. In France, the term "the provinces," which still fuels an outdated revolt against Paris, has fallen into disuse, and yet Paris itself, along with the other major cities, became provincialized during the pandemic, turning into open-air mausoleums or uninhabited movie sets. As we have seen, everyday life tends to neutralize everything, to flatten all that it contains; its space is an indeterminate one that drowns love, feelings, and anger in a colorless gelatine. Hence the strong temptation to double down on it, to accentuate it, the better to thwart it.

There's a charm in letting life take you where it will, in being tossed about like a boat on a river; in life as in poetry, there is a hypnotic power to litany, a bewitchment in repetition and redundancy: after all, the hours of any given day are almost indistinguishable from those of all the other days. But this slight difference is itself already an immense adventure, a thrilling dissonance. What do I care about more events, as long as the new day tells me the same story, apart from a few details? It's like a children's story: even if we already know it, we never tire of its repetition. Especially if the State, in all its benevolence, decides one day to provide us with a universal basic income. We'll end up giving the dates of the calendar and the passing seasons the task of directing and distracting us. There's a sedative pleasure in routine, for it cloaks what had once seemed arbitrary with a veil of necessity. We begin to function automatically, especially when said functioning is punctuated by regular meals, ringing cell phones, video conferences, and flat-screen TV programs. The less eventful our lives are, the more the rare events that do take place acquire an inordinate importance: they come to seem like the magnificent rewards of chance.

Within Romanticism, there was an entire ostentatiousness of boredom, directed against both the busyness of the bourgeoisie and the unrest of the workers. Of all the ills of his century, the one dearest to Musset was this combination of arrogance and minor rebellion. Yawning through life was a way of distinguishing oneself from the degrading toil of the plebs, whether working-class or bourgeois; it meant proclaiming oneself a member of an elite. This form of suffering was different from that of consenting. While the affluent bathed in contentedness, the poet bore witness to his unhappiness and dissidence by way of idleness. Spleen separated this unhappy few from the world of reproduction, bustle, and toil. The boredom they displayed was their trademark and, to be frank, their hysteria. To show the slightest interest in the society of propriety and good manners would have been to make a pact with the enemy. The pale and tormented face of the artist or playwright said: your busybody world doesn't concern me – I'm elsewhere.

Today, faced with a world bristling with threats, we react with a new form of dandyism: we oppose cool to stress, using it as a discreet and effective way of marking our nonconformity. We detach ourselves and drop out, but we do so within everyday life: we become complicit with the latter through a mixture of nonchalance and distance. We bear witness to the tragic aspects of the world without complacency, but also without convulsions, so as to mask our depression or terror. Being cool and pleasant allows us to display positive states of existence without overemphasizing them. We practice the art of disguising emotions as casualness. Our age is full of these falsely indolent people who flaunt detachment, claiming to be the kings of abstention and lack of accomplishment. Their phlegmatic nature is a lesson in a stoicism played in a minor key. They undertake detachment treatments, rejecting in their own way the grandiloquence of their elders, the boomer generation, with all its devotion to the cult of transgression and passion. They have close shaves with the outside world while staying at home and running in place; they disguise their diligence with nonchalance, and convert their anguish into serenity.

Even the crowds mobilizing against climate change, with all their tears and imprecations, ultimately invite everyone to stay at home, so as to practice "demobility" (I borrow the term from French politician Sandrine Rousseau) and "disinnovation." Regardless of the pretexts that are invoked, the result remains the same. The hearth, the house, the commune, and the ZAD[1] become so many variations on the theme of the "home of one's own," the hideout where friends and family can escape the future's uncertainties. This banal refuge conceals a paradox: the more people's lives are ordinary, the more receptive they are to the leitmotif of peril. There is a pleasure in every state of emergency: we experience a paradoxical enjoyment in predicting our own demise. Too many lazy minds disparage Western decadence instead of seeking remedies for our ills. Defeatism is a second home for the privileged; it is the sigh of fat cats purring in comfort. Those who speak of impending doom seek to wake us up, but all they do is numb us. Weather events, outbursts, typhoons, accidents, and attacks enflame our calm existence with an unprecedented thrill. The enemy is among us, watching for our slightest failings. The more order and calm there is, the more we seek to reinforce them. We awake briefly, so as to call for even more torpor; we escape our daily neutrality only to demand an existence that is even more closed off and protected. Sounding the alarm means returning a sense of enchantment to our routines; it allows us to dream of confining ourselves in the face of an imminent cataclysm. The final response is always one of passivity. But when war – the real thing – arrives on our borders, as it did in February 2022, we can no longer afford to mince words: all the excuses disappear; the apocalypse we've predicted a thousand times is upon us, and we must either mobilize or consent to our own disappearance.

98

CHAPTER 15

The Extremists of Routine

In the nineteenth and twentieth centuries, when so many authors sought to expand our feeling of existence, others went even further in the direction of blandness, perfidiously devoting themselves to insisting on the banality of everyday life. I call them *the hardliners of insignificance.* Their tactic of abdication employs the system's own logic. Waging war on nothingness is a delicate and tactical art, especially when the aim is to double down on this nothingness so as to stifle the little that still circulates within it. It's a new form of happiness in reverse: non-life as asceticism; a destiny of nonexistence, a boundless rambling, a boredom so dense that it takes on a fantastic dimension. If heroes are generally in a hurry, experiencing daily life only as a parenthesis between two exploits, this anti-hero experiences only an idle time bordered by long stretches of emptiness. These writers have achieved a real posterity, and are still read by many today, especially among those who resist progress – even if their lineage is not as widely unrecognized as it could be. A testament to this is the Brautigan Library (a homage to the underground writer Richard Brautigan, who committed suicide in 1984 at the age of 49) in Burlington, Vermont, which was made up exclusively of English-language manuscripts rejected by publishers.[1] (The library has since moved to the state of Washington and most of its contents have been digitized.) These gentle rebels didn't say no to the world, settling into the posture of an all-encompassing refusal. Instead, they drifted elsewhere. They hold an important place in the history of negative art. They are not simply the morose accountants of our contemporary hell. Each one's renunciation of life takes on a particular tone, whether in the realm of love, glory, or friendship. What is astonishing is that this little-known literary tradition – what one might call the adventurers of the trifle – still speaks to us today, for it recounts, in words that are often dated, what we have been living through (if in a new setting) for the past few years – and what we could live through again, if, by some misfortune, yet another epidemic were to strike us. These extremists of routine do not mythologize either negation or silence – Rimbaud's silence, severely criticized by Julien Gracq, who recalled that the vow of silence was once the rule when a man of the world left society to die alone. On the contrary, they are committed to an ethics of discretion. To the intoxication of an intense life, they oppose the greyness of a latent life.

They are not failures (to think this would be to judge everything from the standpoint of success), but rather knights of the ellipse, thurifers of limbo. They practice what Florence Lotterie calls an "ethics of absence," and if they appeal to minuscule events (it was the obsession of Surrealism to emphasize tiny miracles, to celebrate fabulous coincidences everywhere), it is not to make epiphanies of them. There exist at least two forms of joy (alongside an infinite variety of misfortunes): one is an expansion that seeks to open all the windows; the other is a contraction that seeks to close them, so as to enjoy a tranquility that the first form of joy sees as uniform and monotonous. The first seeks wonders in the vast world, while the second is content with its domestic microcosm. The enchantment of the open sea versus the small pleasures of the habitual. Most of us oscillate between the two extremes of *the flamboyant and the restricted*, without fitting completely within one or the other. Never has the battle between the spirit of exploration and that of seclusion been as fierce as it is today.

This ironic seismography of Western pettiness combined with a dream of the absolute runs from Henri-Frédéric Amiel to Michel Houellebecq: these writers, separated by 170 years, manifest the same lack of belief in the meaning of life; they belong to a single generation of men who are at once tired and hyperactive, and who record the low-pressure regions of the soul. They are the antidote to the madness of the modern world, with its old revolutionary or technological dreams. Instead of oscillating wildly between burnout and a feeling of nothingness, these disenchanted writers uncompromisingly espouse the option of nullity, claiming to belong to what Gilles Lipovetsky has called the age of emptiness. When one's house becomes a burrow, as in Kafka's story of this name, life for the occupant is reduced to consolidating the den, emphasizing his own buried state, and caring for this hole that allows him to survive. It's the choice between security (at the price of boredom), and freedom (at the price of risk). Life in the burrow is all about making sure he enjoys total peace of mind – even a grain of sand that is out of place brings him into turmoil. Blocking a pathway, plugging a breach: that's his daily routine. A continuous noise, a simple hiss, panics him: is it the precursor to a landslide or of small game digging tunnels? The stronghold is under siege, and because it is a stronghold, it is by definition hostile to others. Since he lives in a burrow, the occupant takes on the mentality of a burrowing mammal: "When autumn sets in, to possess a burrow like mine, and a roof over your head, is great good fortune for anyone getting on in years."[2] The world's hostility to the burrow never ends, and the fight against the outside never ceases. Today, the burrow seems to have become a fictional mass solution.

Consider, for example, the enigmatic opusculum *Theory of Bloom*, written collectively by the trendy ultra-leftist group Tiqqun, which situates itself within a line of descent that includes Oblomov and the character of Leopold Bloom, anti-hero of James Joyce's novel *Ulysses*. *Theory of Bloom* deals with our civilization, which "manages to distract itself from its wreckage by alternating short phases of technophilic hysteria and long periods of contemplative asthenia."[3] The pilgrims of Tiqqun practiced a strange rite every year from 1982 to 1991, holding a "banalysis" conference in the small railway station of Fades in Corrèze. Their claim to fame was to convene meetings in which absolutely nothing happened, in order to experience a reality without interest. The only adventure was that of waiting for delegates to arrive by train, and then incorporating them into the crowd of those already awaiting delegates on the platform, before escorting them back, one by one, for their departure. All complications and incidents that might have broken the marvellous solemnity of this celebration of nothingness were banned. Over the years, the meetings became more festive, with toasts and banquets; people even placed coins on the rails to prove the essential flatness of money. In opposition to social life, which imposes a general rhythm, these banalysts enthusiastically slow their pace almost to a stop, thus altering the path of everyday inertia.

We know that the slide toward dependence, which gives rise to mental contraction, is the curse of old age. Extinguishing life is still an enormous task, as we see in the case of Kafka's "hunger artist," who, locked in a cage under the watchful eye of guards, fasts before an indifferent audience, only to be released in a state of exhaustion. If you want to avoid familiarity with strong emotions, you must be intensely banal, so as to prevent even the slightest rough patch from giving your existence a hint of interest. Emil Cioran, with his usual talent, excoriated "the temptation to exist."[4] How much pride is involved in the attempt not to exist, to rise to the level of nothingness, to say yes to the no, to experience emptiness as a certainty. The renunciation of passions becomes the passion of renunciation. "I'm afraid of dying without having lived," said the moralist Chamfort.[5] "I hope to die without ever having lived," might retort our militants of the very little. Being shriveled is a demanding vocation.

Conclusion

Fall or Transfiguration?

"You cannot invite the wind but you must leave the
window open."

JIDDU KRISHNAMURTI[1]

The Renaissance and the Enlightenment heralded a fertile
time, driven by the promise of better days. Since the end
of the twentieth century, however, we've entered a sterile
era in which a great many factions dream of subjecting
humanity to an imperative of regression. The joyful praise
of existence, curiosity about foreign lands, and freely
wandering the earth have all become suspect. Day after
day, young people are inculcated with lessons in applied
despair. Whence the fierce and divisive battle to define
priorities, as we struggle to decide which of our enemies
we should focus on: global warming, epidemics, terrorism,
or war? From the standpoint of fear, the effect of these
announcements is the same: they all act as enticements to
withdraw from the world, for those who seek, above all,
to protect themselves from the great tragedies of history.

Is it any wonder that the younger generations are plagued by nightmares, no longer believe in the future, and throw themselves headfirst into their burrows to await the end of the world? The need for complete safety can stifle our very desire to be with others. The end of the world is first and foremost the end of the outside world, as the attractiveness of a life lived with other people vanishes. The appetite for life of the 1960s is over: we must discourage everything that is sublime, reduce our ambitions, and invite everyone to orgies of pettiness. The desire to enjoy all that life has to offer is banned, and indeed condemned as a sin against the planet, the nation, the past, morality, and minorities. Over the last few years, how many morose intellectuals and depression merchants have tripped over each other on French airwaves to lecture us and predict terrible punishments? We've spent too much time enjoying ourselves – now it's time to pay!

And so we're encouraged to withdraw into ourselves, for the Outside is an abyss. Inertia is mistaken for prudence. Humanity must be placed under a glass dome. No one can endure the tragedies of our time for long without an escape valve, an excuse to go and hide. One of the most important achievements of freedom, the right to a private life, has thus been inverted: it is now equated with a renunciation of the exercise of public life. Benjamin Constant noted, as early as 1819, that the freedom of the Moderns consisted in "security in private pleasures,"[2] which threatened a massive abstention from politics. And Alexis de Tocqueville, in a famous passage in *Democracy in America*, feared that a muted despotism would invade democratic nations: he spoke of

> an immense and tutelary power [that] likes citizens to enjoy themselves provided that they think only of enjoying themselves. It willingly works for their happiness; but it

wants to be the unique agent and sole arbiter of that; it provides for their security, foresees and secures their needs, facilitates their pleasure, conducts their principal affairs, directs their industry, regulates their estates, divides their inheritances; can it not take away from them entirely the trouble of thinking and the pain of living?[3]

Only when doors and shutters are ajar does the tension between inside and outside become fertile, for this allows movement from one side to the other (the same can be said of borders, which separate people only in order to better connect them). We must oppose to paralyzing anxiety the elegance of assumed risk. It is not when we flee adversity that we become strong. We must say no to the dogmatism of closed versus open and instead insist on porosity – on a proper interval between moderation and bravery, which alone allows creative shocks. We always find our relish for life in the collision between several spheres. As Victor Segalen once said: "I was asked to choose between a hammer and a bell; I confess that I have opted for the sound they made."[4]

It will take both talent and desire for us to continue to live in harmony with our fellow humans, and to fend off the pack of moaners and flagellants. It will take a true renaissance – something we weren't sure the peoples of the West were capable of until recently. The attack on Ukraine started by Moscow on February 24, 2022 caught our old Europe off guard: winded by the pandemic, convinced that universal peace had become the norm and not a Western exception, it nevertheless reacted with solid unanimity. It didn't fold: we were expecting Munich, but instead we got a collective Churchill. In a matter of days, sleeping beauty emerged from the somnambulism that followed the fall of the Berlin Wall. Nations can doze off from time to time, but they can also wake up and emerge stronger from the worst ordeals, offering us admirable examples of resurrection. We're stronger than we think. Our enemies are weaker than they think. A fine rebuttal for those bards of decline who revel in our abjection and predict our imminent demise.

But we must remain cautious. War, like disease, is an ambiguous master that can stupefy us just as much as it awakens us. The telluric shock provoked by the Russian invasion of Ukraine, and the extraordinary solidarity shown in its wake, may not survive the test of time – not to mention rising gas and oil prices, runaway inflation, the terror of a nuclear threat, and our multitude of daily worries. Slippers mean comfort, but they also mean cold feet – a reluctance to do what we must. We've gone so far as to reopen coal mines, with little regard for our ideals of sobriety. Once our enthusiasm has died down, what will be left of our little burst of compassion? We'll be highly tempted to impose peace on Ukraine at any price to avoid a larger conflict, and tyrants will view this peace as an abdication on the part of the civilized world. Freedom often comes at a price that is too high for wealthy nations, who forswore war and are now haunted by it like a nightmare. The battle, which is taking place on multiple fronts, requires two virtues in particular: endurance and perseverance. The stakes are the same as they were in 1939 and the Cold War, and just as immense: will democracies bend to power or stand up against barbarism?

It is also possible that Oblomov will return to his original homeland, Russia, which is now plagued by nihilism and violence. It is possible that the Russian people, stricken with impotence and fear, will, aside from a few remarkable dissidents, hide themselves away in a burrow of sorts, thus confirming the Marquis de Custine's frightening observation in 1839: "It may be said of the Russians, great and small, that they are drunk with slavery."[5] It is not out of the question that the Despot will be overthrown one day and replaced by a more conciliatory team that will put an end to the war, for want of overturning the age-old absolutism of the Russian Federation.

The question of who will prevail, both here and there, between the apostles of capitulation and the partisans of resistance, remains open. We must put our trust in future generations. If there are some young people who snivel and act like victims, there are others who are making a stand, and who intend to shape the future rather than simply putting up with it.

The die is not yet cast.

But if we give in, we're lost.

Notes

Preface: The Oblomov Hypothesis

1 Ivan Goncharov, *Oblomov*, trans. David Magarshack, Penguin, 1954, p. 14.
2 Ibid., p.14.
3 Ibid., p. 71.
4 Ibid., p. 183.
5 Ibid., p. 184.
6 Ibid., p. 62.
7 Ibid., p. 231.
8 Ibid., p. 184.
9 Ibid., p. 186.
10 Ibid., p. 466.

1 The Four Horsemen of the Apocalypse …

1 Translator's note: Greta Thunberg's speech can be found here: www.theguardian.com/environment/2019/jan/25/our-house-is-on-fire-greta-thunberg16-urges-leaders-to-act-on-climate.

2 The Bankruptcy of Eros?

1 See the petition "Une inquiétante présomption de culpabilité s'invite trop souvent en matière d'infractions sexuelles,"

initiated by Delphine Meillet and Marie Dose, in *Le Monde*, March 8, 2020. [Unless otherwise stated, all translations from languages other than English are made by the translator.]
2 In *C'est fatigant, la liberté . . . Une leçon de la crise* (Éditions de l'Observatoire, 2021), Jean-Claude Kaufmann notes that, during the first lockdown, the erotic life of French people collapsed, and the desire to come together disappeared (p. 46). It remains to be seen whether this desire will return . . .

3 Forbidden Travel?

1 Blaise Pascal, *Pensées*, trans. Roger Ariew, Hackett, 2004, pp. 38–9.
2 Translator's note: See, for example, Nicolas Massol, "Les écolos, croquemitaines de l'aviation," *Libération*, April 4, 2021.
3 Translator's note: Tennessee Williams, *One Arm and Other Stories*, New Directions, 1948, p. 84.
4 Once more, see his *C'est fatigant, la liberté . . .*
5 Translator's note: Arthur Rimbaud, *Complete Works*, trans. Paul Schmidt, Harper Perennial, 2000, p. 228, translation modified.

4 Is a Banal Life Worth Living?

1 See his excellent book *Éloge du quotidien, essai sur la peinture hollandaise du XVIIe siècle*, Seuil, 2009.
2 Here, I take up an argument that I dealt with to a lesser degree in *L'Euphorie perpétuelle*, Grasset, 2000.
3 Pascal Bruckner, *The Temptation of Innocence: Living in the Age of Entitlement*, Algora, 2000, p. 44; Alain Ehrenberg, *La Fatigue d'être soi*, Odile Jacob, 1998.
4 Joyce Carol Oates has written a short story based on this painting, "The Woman in the Window," in which two adulterous lovers plan to meet in a room and each, overwhelmed by hatred, prepares to kill the other. See *One Story* 217 (June 9, 2016).

5 The Bovarysme of the Cell Phone

1 Emmanuel Levinas, *De l'Existence à l'existant*, Vrin, 1981, p. 38.
2 See Neil Postman, *Amusing Ourselves to Death: Public Discourse in the Age of Show Business*, Penguin, 1985; and Bruno Patino, *La Civilisation du poisson rouge*, Grasset, 2019.

6 Cave, Cell, and Bedroom

1 Plato, *Republic*, Book VII, 516b–517b.
2 See Bernard Edelman, *La Maison de Kant*, Payot, 1984, pp. 25–6.
3 See Eric Sutter, *Code et langage des sonneries de cloches en Occident*, SFC, 2006.
4 See Todorov, *Éloge du quotidien*, p. 29.
5 Saint Jean Cassien, *Les Institutions cénobitiques*, Éditions du Cerf, 1965 [AD 420], cited in Madeleine Bouchez, *L'Ennui, de Sénèque à Moravia*, Bordas, 1973, p. 34.
6 See Pier Vittorio Aureli, *Less Is Enough*, Strelka Press, 2013.
7 Saint Augustine, *Confessions*, trans. Henry Chadwick, Oxford University Press, 1991, p. 43 (3.6.11).
8 Translator's note: Jean-Jacques Rousseau, *Confessions*, trans. Angela Scholar, Oxford University Press, 2008, p. 110.

7 The Beauty of One's Own Home

1 Michelle Perrot, *The Bedroom: An Intimate History*, trans. Lauren Elkin, Yale University Press, 2018, p. 14.
2 Cited in ibid., p. 37.
3 Virginia Woolf, *A Room of One's Own*, Harcourt, 1929, p. 4.
4 Michel de Montaigne, *The Complete Essays*, trans. M. A. Screech, Penguin, 1991, p. 270.

8 The Torments and Delights of a Life in Shackles

1 Charles Baudelaire, "The Double Room," in *Paris Spleen*, trans. Louise Varèse, New Directions, 1947, p. 5.
2 Ibid., p. 6.
3 Translator's note: Bruckner is referring here to what is known in French as the ZAD or "Zone à défendre" (zone to defend) which, per Wikipedia, refers to "a militant occupation that is intended to physically blockade a development project." The most famous is that of Notre-Dame-des-Landes, which began in 2012 to oppose the construction of an airport, and where about 200 people still live, despite the abandonment of the project in 2018.
4 Jean-Jacques Rousseau, *The Reveries of the Solitary Walker*, trans. Charles E. Butterworth, Hackett, 1992, p. 62.
5 Ibid., p. 63.
6 Ibid., p. 69.
7 Quoted in *A History of Private Life*, vol. IV: *From the Fires of Revolution to the Great War*, ed. Michelle Perrot, trans. Arthur Goldhammer, Harvard University Press, 1990, p. 356.
8 Translator's note: Gaston Bachelard, *The Right to Dream*, trans. J. A. Underwood, Dallas Institute Publications, 1988, p. 83.
9 Annie Ernaux, *Exteriors*, trans. Tanya Leslie, Seven Stories Press, 1996, p. 91.
10 See Emanuele Coccia, *Philosophie de la maison*, Rivages, 2021, p. 186.
11 Gustave Flaubert, *Bouvard and Pécuchet*, trans. A. J. Krailsheimer, Penguin, 1976, p. 31.

9 The Land of Sleep: Hypnos and Thanatos

1 Translator's note: see his novel *Grey Bees*, trans. Boris Dralyuk, Deep Vellum, 2022.
2 See Guillaume Garnier, *L'Oubli des peines. Une histoire du sommeil*, Presses Universitaires de Rennes, 2013. In his study

Montaillou: The Promised Land of Error (trans. Barbara Bray, Vintage, 1979), Emmanuel Le Roy Ladurie evokes the hour of first sleep and the habit of dividing the night into several segments.

3 Translator's note: Georges Perec, *A Man Asleep*, trans. Andrew Leak, in Perec, *Things: A Story of the Sixties and A Man Asleep*, David R. Godine, 1990, p. 161.

4 Translator's note: Ismail Kadare, *The Palace of Dreams*, trans. Barbara Bray, Arcade, 2011.

5 Translator's note: Marcel Proust, *The Captive*, trans. C. K. Scott Moncrieff and Terence Kilmartin, Random House, 1993, p. 520.

6 Translator's note: ibid., pp. 84–5.

10 Digital Wonderland or the Triumph of Slouching?

1 Albert O. Hirschman, *Shifting Involvements: Private Interests and Public Action*, Princeton University Press, 2002 [p. 62].

2 Translator's note: see Michel Serres, *Thumbelina: The Culture and Technology of Millennials*, trans. Daniel W. Smith, Rowman & Littlefield, 2014.

3 Translator's note: Hannah Arendt, *Between Past and Future: Six Exercises in Political Thought*, Viking, 1961, p. 4.

4 Translator's note: Fernando Pessoa, *The Book of Disquiet*, trans. Richard Zenith, Penguin, 2003, p. 254.

5 Friedrich Nietzsche, *Beyond Good and Evil*, trans. Marion Faber, Oxford University Press, 2009, § 26.

11 Diderot's Dressing Gown

1 Cited in Hirschman, *Shifting Involvements*, p. 53.

2 See Juliette Garnier, "'Tout le monde n'aura pas sa charentaise sous le sapin,'" *Le Monde*, December 2, 2021.

3 See Luc-Michel Fouassier's delicious little novel *Les Pantoufles* [*The Slippers*], Folio Gallimard, 2020, which won the Prix des Libraires *Télérama*.

4 Translator's note: G. W. F. Hegel, *Phenomenology of Spirit*, trans. A. V. Miller, Oxford University Press, 1977, p. 404.
5 Denis Diderot, "Regrets on Parting with My Old Dressing Gown," trans. Kate Tunstall and Katie Scott, *Oxford Art Journal* 39.2 (2016), pp. 175–84, here pp. 177–8.
6 Brian Fagan and Nadia Durrani, *What We Did in Bed: A Horizontal History*, Yale University Press, 2019, p. 158.
7 Levinas, *De l'Existence à l'existant*, p. 60.
8 See Charlotte Bozonnet, "Raymond Depardon et Kamel Daoud croisent leurs regards sur l'Algérie d'hier et d'aujourd'hui," *Le Monde*, February 19, 2022.

12 Those Who Have Deserted Modernity

1 Translator's note: see Houellebecq's poem "Midday" in his *Unreconciled: Poems 1991–2013*, trans. Gavin Bowd, Farrar, Straus and Giroux, 2017, pp. 23–4.
2 Xavier de Maistre, *A Journey around My Room*, trans. Andrew Brown, Hesperus, 2004, p. 4.
3 Ibid., p. 7.
4 Ibid., p. 21.
5 See Frédéric Beigbeider, *Bibliothèque de survie*, L'Observatoire, 2021, pp. 125–6.
6 De Maistre, *A Journey around My Room*, p. 67.
7 Translator's note: Herman Melville, "Bartleby, the Scrivener: A Story of Wall-Street," in *Melville's Short Novels*, ed. Dan McCall, W. W. Norton & Company, 2002, p. 10.

13 Weather Sorrow

1 Quoted from volume XII of Amiel's *Journal intime*, L'Âge d'Homme, 1984.
2 See Anouchka Vasak, "Grandes Émotions météorologiques collectives," in *Histoire des émotions*, vol. II, ed. Alain Corbin, Seuil Histoire, 2016, pp. 115–16.

14 Existential Defeatism

1 Translator's note: see my note on this term in chapter 8.

15 The Extremists of Routine

1 See Enrique Vila-Matas, *Bartleby & Co.*, trans. Jonathan Dunne, New Directions, 2004, p. 37.

2 Franz Kafka, "The Burrow," in *The Complete Stories*, ed. Nahum N. Glatzer, Schocken, 1995, p. 327.

3 Tiqqun, *Theory of Bloom*, trans. Robert Hurley, Ill Will Editions, 1999, p. 1.

4 See E. M. Cioran, *The Temptation to Exist*, trans. Richard Howard, Arcade, 2013.

5 Translator's note: Nicolas Chamfort, *Products of the Perfected Civilization*, trans. W. S. Merwin, Macmillan, 1969, p. 107.

Conclusion: Fall or Transfiguration?

1 Translator's note: Jiddu Krishnamurti, *Freedom from the Known*, ch. 16. See jiddu-krishnamurti.net/en/freedom-from -the-known/1968-00-00-jiddu-krishnamurti-freedom-from -the-known-chapter-16.

2 Translator's note: Benjamin Constant, "The Liberty of the Ancients Compared with That of the Moderns," in *Political Writings*, ed. and trans. Biancamaria Fontana, Cambridge University Press, 1988, p. 317.

3 Alexis de Tocqueville, *Democracy in America*, trans. Harvey C. Mansfield and Delba Winthrop, University of Chicago Press, 2000, p. 663.

4 Translator's note: Victor Segalen, *Équipée*, in *Oeuvres Complètes*, ed. Henri Bouillier, Robert Laffont, 1995, vol. II, p. 318, my trans.

5 Translator's note: Astolphe de Custine, *Letters from Russia*, ed. Anka Muhlstein, New York Review Books, 2002, p. 102.